The Branch and the Vine

A Midweek Prayer Series
By Frank Phillips

Written into book form
By Dan Augsburger

To Order: Write: Justified Walk Ministries,
PO Box 233 Berrien Springs, MI 49103-0233
Call: (269)471-9224
E-mail: justifiedwalk@justifiedwalk.com
This edition of the book is not for sale.

It is provided without cost as a result of the sacrificial giving of many individuals whose lives have been changed by the Lord Jesus through the content of this book! In light of the lateness of the hour and the urgency of the message contained, we are attempting to distribute this book as broadly and as quickly as possibly. If you have been blessed by what you have read, we pray that you will share this book with someone else, and we will happily supply another copy. You are also welcome to make up to 1,000 copies of this edition of the book for non-commercial study and sharing purposes, provided the book is identically reproduced; copies are provided free, and there is no minimum shipping or handling fee. Though permission is given to make copies, the text is copyrighted and all rights are retained. Donations to support this effort are gratefully accepted should the Lord put a burden on your heart for such a donation. They are also tax deductible.

"Freely have ye received; freely give."
"It is in giving that we receive."

Copyright 2009 by Dan Augsburger
ISBN: 0-982597-20-7
Edited by Dan Augsburger
 (path2prayer@yahoo.com; www.path2prayer.com)
Layout and Design: Margie Mitchell/Son Praises Graphic Design
Cover Design: Larry Crum
All Bible texts are the King James Version unless otherwise specified. You may order, read, or listen to this and other sermons CDs, books, and handouts from the work of Frank Phillips on the internet at: www.JustifiedWalk.com. You may find additional resources on prayer and achieving victory at www.path2prayer.com or at www.justifiedwalk.com.

TABLE OF CONTENTS

Chapter 1	Abiding and Dependency	5
Chapter 2	Abiding and Pruning	18
Chapter 3	Abiding and Daily Living	33
Chapter 4	Abiding "As I"	47
Chapter 5	Abiding and Reflecting Christ's Character	63
Chapter 6	Abiding and Unlimited Joy	81

PREFACE

Preparing Pastor Frank Phillips' The Branch and the Vine prayer meeting series for publication has been a labor of friendship, appreciation for his ministry, the outcome of thirty years of thinking on the subject and listening to many of his series on cassette, and corresponding with Elder Phillips for several years.

I first became acquainted with Pastor Phillips in 1978 during the course of a week of prayer he gave at Andrews University at my invitation. Popularly known as the Justified Walk series, it was a great blessing to many people. Unfortunately the series title was never his preferred choice-I had provided the title since he had not supplied one-because, in his words, his series was about transformation, which included justification and sanctification.

We became friends through the week, and began trading letters after he left. In the course of that exchange, he sent me an unpublished manuscript and cassettes of several meetings, including one set entitled The Branch and the Vine, which he felt was particularly important.

The manuscript was eventually published as His Robe Or Mine. Focusing on the need to die to self, the book significantly advanced the understanding of what it means to die to self. Thousands have read that book and are rejoicing in a newfound desire and power to serve Jesus.

However, because the abiding or indwelling portion of that message was only minimally touched upon in His Robe Or Mine, I often wished there were a fuller treatment of the abiding/indwelling part of the message. That fuller treatment is provided in The Branch and the Vine, and perhaps explains why he thought that particular series was so important.

In editing the The Branch and the Vine transcript, I was constantly aware that many people would have already listened to the series and would be aware of differences, and that some day I would be talking with Elder Phillips about his series and wanted him to be pleased with the outcome. I accordingly tried to make sure the book continued to reflect his thoughts and achieve his objectives, and therefore neither added to, nor took away from, what he said. Neither did I make explanatory notes, preferring readers seek to understand the concepts for themselves.

I am pleased to report that early feedback suggests this book not only provides more insight, but is considered by many to be a necessary sequel to His Robe Or Mine. It is with joy, therefore, that The Branch and the Vine is published, knowing that thousands will potentially find in it additional secrets on how to live for Jesus.

Many individuals have contributed to making this book possible, including the ladies who did the original transcripts, Elder Phillips' daughter Alice, and those who work at Justified Walk Ministries, numerous proof readers and countless volunteers. Thank you for the important role each of you have played. Thank you, most of all to Jesus for the difference He has made through Elder Phillips' books in so many of our lives.

Dan Augsburger

Path2Prayer Ministries - (path2prayer.com; path2prayer@yahoo.com)

Chapter 1

Abiding and Dependency

It's a little difficult to explain how ministers of the Gospel decide what message God would have them share. And I can assure you that during the past few weeks since we concluded the last series of Wednesday night meetings, I have been praying and searching and asking the Lord to lead us to the message we need to understand more than anything else.

The Most Important Truths

During the past three weeks as I have been earnestly asking the Lord to lead me to the right message, over and over I have been drawn back to Christ's message to His disciples on that last Thursday night. In John 14, 15, 16, and 17 you find enough to preach about from now till we get into the Kingdom of Heaven, and there is no end to it. My mind would constantly go back to the thought: If you only had two or three hours to give the message that you wanted to give, what message would it be? Would you waste time in useless prittle-prattle? Obviously not! Every word, every thought, would be vitally important. And so, in coming back to these chapters, my mind was directed particularly to the fact that in John 15:1-8 the Lord Jesus attempted to use an illustration—not a parable, not a story—an illustration to teach in a nutshell the most important truths that God has ever given mankind.

The truths given in these eight verses are so clearly illustrated that it is absolutely impossible to misunderstand them. You either have to completely ignore this illustration or believe it. There is no other way around it. You can't possibly misunderstand it. You can ignore it, pick up other verses of Scripture along the way and come up with other conclusions, but you cannot possibly misunderstand this illustration. In spite of this fact, we find ourselves pushing it to the side and picking up other verses of Scripture that will substantiate, or at least attempt to substantiate, our preconceived opinions.

These eight verses of Scripture are going to be the foundation of our studies for the next couple of weeks. Here Jesus said:

> *"I am the True Vine and My Father is the Husbandman. Every branch in Me that beareth not fruit He taketh away; and every branch that beareth fruit He purgeth it, that it may bring forth more fruit. Now ye are clean through the word which I have spoken unto you. Abide in Me, and I in you. As the branch cannot bear fruit of itself, except it abide in the vine; no more can ye, except ye abide in Me. I am the Vine, ye are the branches: He that abideth in Me, and I in him, the same bringeth forth much fruit: for without Me ye can do nothing. If a man abide not in Me, he is cast forth as a branch, and is withered; and men gather them, and cast them into the fire, and they are burned. If ye abide in Me, and My words abide in you, ye shall ask what ye will, and it shall be done unto you. Herein is My Father glorified, that ye bear much fruit; so shall ye be My disciples"* (John 15:1-8).

In these verses of Scripture there is very interesting material that could keep us studying for a long time. Outstanding truths brought to light include, a Vine, a Husbandman, branches, fruit, abiding, and discipleship.

Notice also that the illustrations Jesus gave were always clear and to the point. Sometimes the parables are a bit difficult to understand—for example, the parable that Jesus gave of the rich man and Lazarus. In some parables the exact message being communicated is hard to pinpoint. But the illustrations that Jesus used were clear and simple. For example, when He was out in the field and said, "Consider the lilies of the field, how they grow; they neither toil nor spin," it was impossible to miss the point!

But sometimes truths spoken in such clear terms, with such simple language, become difficult to understand because of the challenge of practically applying them in general, or applying them to a particular set of circumstances. This is where the difficulty emerges. If we are having difficulty in practically applying a truth, we backpedal, saying, "Well maybe He didn't mean this," and seek to justify our actions by attempting to water down the simplicity of the truth.

Abiding: The Main Topic

When I ask a group of people, "What is the main topic of these first eight verses?" various suggestions are made. I hear about implied promises, the Vine, abiding, producing fruit, what the illustration teaches about having a relationship with Christ, our inability to do anything on our own, discipleship, and the possibility of having false vines since there is a True Vine. Eventually one comes to the conclusion, however, that the main topic is *abiding*!—what it means to actually abide in Christ.

What about this business of "abiding"? How many times have you said, "How is this 'abiding in Christ' accomplished? How do I actually abide in Christ every day of my life? How do I continue abiding?" Understanding how to abide becomes a major question, because if we don't understand how abiding is initiated, how can we understand how abiding continues?

Turn with me to 2 Corinthians 1:21, 22. Paul said, "Now He which stablisheth us with you in Christ . . ." What did he say? . . . He which stablisheth us with you in Christ, and hath anointed us, is . . . who? "God"! God does this; God places us in Christ. He not only places us in Christ, but then He actually follows through.

Now notice verse 22: "Who hath also sealed us, and given the earnest of the Spirit in our hearts." God puts us into Christ, anoints us in Christ, and then tells us that instead of our doing this, it is the Holy Spirit who is doing it. The Holy Spirit puts us in Christ, keeps us in Christ, and then seals us.

What about this sealing? When anything is sealed, it is sealed because there is an essential time element. Isn't that true? When you seal a jar of fruit there is a time element that you are concerned about, for it will spoil if you don't seal it. When you have a document notarized and sealed, it is because there is a time element involved. You know about it at that moment, but you want somebody else, at some future time, to also know about it being a fact. So there is always a time element involved.

Abiding: A Continuing Process

Let's get to purging. Instead of answering what purging is, for the time being let us limit our understanding of purging as being a continuing process. Purging is not an *after* kind of thing; it is a *while* thing. Purging takes place *while* other things are going on. Here is the actual process: The purpose of a branch is to bear *fruit*; purging makes it bear *more fruit*; more purging makes it bear *much fruit*. So you go from fruit, to more fruit, to much fruit, and Jesus said that His plan for you and for me is to bear much fruit. So a lot of purging is going to take place along the way. This is absolutely a fact, because when the Gardener—the Husbandman—sees the branch and recognizes that it needs a little pruning here and there, He goes ahead with the pruning whether the branch likes it or not.

Abiding: An Anointing

Now turn with me to another verse of Scripture that will carry this thought a step further. Now remember, ". . . He which stablisheth us with you in Christ, and hath anointed us, is God; Who hath also sealed us, and given us the earnest of the Spirit in our hearts" (2 Corinthians 1:21, 22). So not only are we established and anointed in Christ, but God also seals and grants the Holy Spirit to dwell in our hearts.

Now turn to 1 John 2:27, 28. "But the anointing which ye have received of Him abideth in you . . ." Notice the anointing is there again, "But the anointing which ye have received of Him" . . .—Of whom? God! John says this anointing is of God. "But the anointing which ye have received of Him abideth in you, and ye need not that any man teach you." Isn't that interesting? "Ye need not that any man teach you." Why? Because the Holy Spirit will.

The person who is honestly and consistently abiding in Christ will be constantly receiving his instructions from the Holy Spirit—he is constantly being taught! It isn't a matter of some man coming along and teaching; rather it is a matter of receiving instruction from the Holy Spirit. Now notice, "But as the same anointing teacheth you of all things, and is truth, and is no lie, and even as it hath taught you, ye shall abide in . . . whom? "Him." "Ye shall abide in Him!" Now verse 28: "And now, little children, abide in Him; that, when He shall appear, we may have confidence, and not be ashamed before Him at His coming." Jesus said, "Abide in Me." Can you see that there is much solemn truth involved in this abiding business?

What does this abiding do for us? Why does God want us to abide in Christ? Why is this whole thing given to us? 1 John 2:6 says, "He that saith he abideth in Him ought himself also so to walk, even as He walked." Abiding enables a person to "walk, even as He walked."

Keeping this in mind, let's return to John 15:5, where John is quoting the words of Jesus when He said "I am the Vine; ye are the branches: He that abideth in Me, and I in him, the same bringeth forth much fruit: for without Me ye can do nothing!" We already touched on the fact that the branch has only one purpose: bearing fruit! The branch is the portion of the vine that bears the fruit—the illustration is absolutely crystal clear. Yet we need to establish a bit more of a foundation about what is accomplished before we get into the profound yet simple truths of the illustration.

Abiding and Fruit-bearing

Now what does this abiding do so far as fruit-bearing is concerned? Well, we go back to 1 John 3:6, where it says, "Whosoever abideth in Him sinneth not"! What do you think of that? That's beyond your comprehension and mine, isn't it? "Whosoever abideth in Him sinneth not"! Now tell me, Why is this a fact, and how is this a fact? Is this about pardon? Is this about believing in it? Well, how much can the branch do that abides in the vine? It can do nothing! The branch that abides in the vine can do nothing! How much? Nothing! All it can do is abide; that's all it does. It is true that it receives its strength from the vine, but does it say, "Well, now, I'd like to have five gallons of sap today"? Or does it say, "I only need a quart today!"? Does it? No! What does the branch do? Nothing! It receives exactly what the vine gives it!

Now the word "abiding" implies something very important for us to understand. What is implied when the word "abiding" is used in the Scriptures? What is implied when the word "abide" is used as a command? The point is this: There would be no need to give the counsel—the command—to abide if it were not the natural thing to do the opposite! Isn't that true? The natural thing is to not abide. We get the information; we gather the facts and then go our way with a big smile on our face. Isn't that what we do; get the inspiration, then leave the Source? That's the natural thing to do. Jesus said "Abide." This abiding, then, is the essential thing, the absolutely essential thing, for living the

Christian life. Abiding is the one thing that we must absolutely do to live the victorious life; there is no way around it.

Now immediately somebody says, "But tell me, how?" Notice page 69 of *Steps to Christ*: "Do you ask, 'How am I to abide in Christ?'" Have you ever asked that? Absolutely! "In the same way as you received Him at first. 'As ye have therefore received Christ Jesus the Lord, so walk ye in Him.'" (Col. 2:6) So, if we abide in Christ, the ability to walk even as He walked is ours. Isn't that right? Of course it is. That's why 1 John 2:6 says that the ability to walk only comes as we abide.

Abiding: Constantly Accepting

Now the author says quoting Paul, "As ye have therefore received Christ, so walk. . . ." There's nothing different about abiding than actually receiving Him. Just as you *accepted* Christ initially, abiding in Him is *constantly accepting*! And when we accepted Christ in the very first place, self was simply—to the very best of our knowledge at least—set aside, and we accepted Him in His full Person to the point that He actually revealed Himself to us.

The problem, you see, is that as we go along in life, He reveals Himself in greater measure, and therefore there are greater demands on our lives because we are actually supposed to be able to abide and conform to His pattern. And that's exactly what the branch does. The branch does nothing but bear the leaves, which enable the chemical processes to take place, taking the sap from the vine and producing fruit. But the branch doesn't put any effort into it. It doesn't because it was made to bear fruit! You and I were made to bear fruit for God; to reflect His image—that's what He made us for from the very beginning. Now notice, this is only possible in an effortless —and I mean exactly that—in an effortless manner! The problem is that abiding, and fruit-bearing, and works, get all mixed up in our thinking.

Abiding: Giving and Taking

The author goes on to say quoting Paul, "As ye have therefore received Christ Jesus the Lord, so walk ye in Him." "The just shall live by faith." "You gave yourself to God, to be His wholly, to serve and obey Him, and you took Christ as your Saviour."[1] And there's not a person taking in these words that hasn't done that, I believe. "You could not yourself atone for your sins or change your heart; but having given yourself to God, you believe that He for Christ's sake did all this for you."

I know you believe this; there is no question about this in your mind. "By *faith* you became Christ's, and by faith you are to grow up in Him—by giving and taking." By what? "By giving and taking." Is that what the branch does? Yes. What does the branch take? It takes the sap from the Vine; it also takes the sunshine from the same Source—from God. It's constantly taking. And then what does it do in turn? "By giving *and* taking." Now notice. "You are to *give* all,—your heart, your will, your service,—give yourself to Him to obey all His requirements; *and* you must *take* all."

But notice, the *Vine* determines the amount! And just the amount the Vine is ready to give, is the amount we are to take. Why? Because that's the amount the Vine knows we need in order to bear the particular kind of fruit we're supposed to bear.

Now notice: ". . . and you must *take* all,—Christ, the fullness of all blessing, to abide in your heart, to be your Strength, your Righteousness, your everlasting Helper,—to give you power to obey."[2]

Now if we abide, we are to walk even as He walked. But we are not to walk in our own strength. We are to walk in His strength because He abides and He gives us the power to actually walk even as He walked. It isn't something that we can do by effort—not in any sense of the word.

Abiding is without question the most difficult state of the Christian life. It is not difficult for me to surrender my life to Christ. It is not difficult for me to accept Christ. But to abide is very difficult.

Now can you think of any reasons why this is so? Probably one of the greatest reasons is that most of us try to make this a mental act. But notice, while the surrender that comes when I first accept Christ is a mental process, for God appeals to my thinking mind and I accept Him mentally, abiding goes deeper and affects one of the most difficult parts of our living. Did you ever have to wait for your wife while she was shopping? It was difficult to "abide" while she was shopping, wasn't it? You stood there gritting your teeth and saying, "Why is it taking her so long to buy a pair of shoes?" And this can be just as hard for a lady as a man. She says, "Why does it take you so long to shave, anyway?"

Waiting for the Lord, letting something rest with Him is also a very, very difficult thing. Why? Because it touches the emotional part of our being, not just the intellect. It would help if we could honestly say while waiting, "Of course I would want to be particular, too, if I were in there buying a pair of shoes." But we don't respond like that; we simply feel hurt in our emotions and get all tense. You see, the real problem is that abiding touches the feelings.

Abiding and the Spirit's Fruit

How, then, does the branch produce perfect fruit? What is our work? It is always—and I emphasize this again—it's always to abide and let the Vine do the work. Now this is absolutely difficult for us to understand. If we abide and let God do the work, then it is done right, and we become channels through whom He can flow. If we put ourselves into it, we mess things up; and we've been messing things up for 6,000 years, which is why it is taking us so long.

We're talking about fruit-bearing, but what kind of fruit are we talking about? Fruit-bearing is actually a matter of bearing the fruit of the Spirit described in the book of Galatians: love, joy, peace, long-suffering, gentleness, goodness, faith, meekness, and temperance.

Lack of Abiding and Withered Branches

Staying with the illustration, Jesus said, "I am the True Vine, you are the branches, and My Father is the Husbandman." We must constantly keep these three elements in mind; if we forget, we will get completely lost. Now remember, this is the simplest type of illustration; you could not find any simpler illustration than the branch and the Vine. John 15:6 tells us, "If a man abide not in Me, he is cast forth as a branch, and is withered; and men gather them, and cast them into the fire, and they are burned." The branch that is not an abiding branch is only fit to be burned; it is worthless—totally and completely worthless!

Now someone asks, How do you correlate being worthless with the fact that if you don't abide, you do other works? Remember, you are dealing with the fruit of the Spirit, which is an unnatural thing. The natural thing is to do what Satan naturally does in us. So, we are either bearing the fruit Satan gives us or bearing the fruit God gives us.

Now turn with me to Galatians 5:17. We find there the contrast between the fruit and the works that we have been talking about. In this verse the matter of "works" comes up. It says in Galatians 5:17: "For the flesh lusteth against the Spirit, and the Spirit against the flesh: and these are contrary the one to the other: so that ye cannot do the things that ye would." It's entirely impossible! There's only one way it can be done, and that is to rest, completely abiding in Christ.

Abiding and the Fruit-bearing Environment

Now notice verses 19-21. "Now the works of the flesh are manifest, which are these; Adultery, fornication, uncleanness, lasciviousness, idolatry, witchcraft, hatred, variance, emulations, wrath, strife, seditions, heresies, envyings, murders, drunkenness, revelings, and such like: of the which I tell you before, as I have also told you in times past, that they which do such things shall not inherit the Kingdom of God." These are the natural things to do, and there are many variations. But the thing we want to establish is the need for the branch and the Vine to be tied together very, very closely. But what is it that most often separates the Vine from the branch? Is it self? Neglect? Pruning? Sin? What comes between the Vine and the branch? Would you be surprised if I told you the thing that really comes between the Vine and the branch is fruit? Yes, fruit, the very thing the branch is intended for, comes between the Vine and the branch. And God ordained that the branch would only bear fruit, and made the branch for that purpose. But the very thing God intended is the very thing that separates the Vine from the branch.

The problem, you see, is that we are branches. Did you ever hear a branch saying, "I'd like to bear apples this time, even though I'm a peach tree"? "I think I want to bear apricots this time"? Or, being realistic, somebody says, "Well, so far as this business of fruit-bearing goes, it's OK, but you don't understand my situation. If you had to live where I live, with whom I live, you would understand why I can't bear fruit in this situation!" Did you ever hear anyone say, "You simply can't bear fruit in this situation"? Listen, what branch, even though it were in the middle of an orchard, would say, "Look, I could bear fruit if I were out in the open fields somewhere."

The need is to learn how to successfully bear fruit in whatever environment we find ourselves. Imagine a branch being completely separated—divided—from the Vine. Why? Because the branch comes to a point where it says, "I can't bear fruit in my situation." Many individuals I have talked with say, "Well, if you had to work where I work, you would understand why I can't bear fruit." I've heard them say,

"You are a preacher, and you go around talking to people that are very, very easy to work with. So it's easy for you to bear fruit. But if you had to work with the kind of people I have to work with—cursing, swearing, you know, all the things that go on—you would have a difficult time too." Or, "If you had a family like I have, the kids would tear you apart. Day after day they are into all kinds of mischief. Just imagine if you had to put up with that kind of thing." But *the environment the branch finds itself in has absolutely nothing to do with fruit-bearing*—it has nothing to do with it at all. An apple tree will still be an apple tree even if it is in the middle of quince trees. It doesn't have to conform and say, "I'd better work at being a quince this time"; it doesn't have to. But we do? Finding ourselves in a difficult environment, we feel compelled to conform. So we come up with excuses for not bearing fruit; but they are only excuses.

Abiding, Trials, and Fruit-bearing

The branch only does what comes naturally. Do blossoms put any effort into pollinating? No, they wait for the God of Heaven to also take care of the pollinating. There's not any effort. They simply bear the blossoms, and the pollination takes place through God's working upon that flower—through His Own way, whether it means the pollination being carried by bees, the wind, or something else. The plant still grows perfectly normal, and doesn't put any effort into the process. We must accept God's simple lesson, and get over the notion that environment affects our ability to bear fruit.

One person asked, "What if wind, a storm, cold, or some other abnormal situation comes along? How would that affect fruit-bearing?" Fruit-bearing would undoubtedly be affected to some degree, but I don't exactly know how to relate to that, nor do I think we have to factor in all the abnormalities in order to use it as a practical illustration, because the illustration is still true: God is still responsible for the fruit-bearing!

Please also note that the abiding here is more than sitting down and doing nothing physiologically. Don't get the idea that you can only sit in a pew at church, and then go home and sit in a rocker before the fireplace.

Waiting—abiding, trusting—is a condition of the emotions. Intellectually I accept Christ, but to abide there is all about the emotions—which is where the real problem actually takes place.

The Lord doesn't prune until there is fruit. Let me repeat that: The Lord doesn't prune until there is fruit! If He were to start pruning before there were any fruit, it would hurt. And we might react and say, "I'm through with this!" But when there is fruit, He prunes, and then there is more fruit. And then He prunes more. I can hear someone saying, "But that's not what I wanted. I don't want any more of this stuff that hurts!" But God keeps pruning, and finally there is much fruit. And all of it comes while I am abiding. So the individual who abides is not only abiding in moments of ease, but also abiding through trials and perplexities.

So we come back to the same thing: Our environment has nothing to do with our fruit-bearing or with our abiding. We abide simply and completely and wholly *in spite* of the environment. We get back to this fact repeatedly, because we make so many excuses for lack of fruit on account of the environment we live in or because of the particular situations we find ourselves in. Even in the case of tornado-like trials, God takes responsibility for the perplexities and trials that seem to come from outside factors. We come up with these excuses for not bearing fruit. And remember, when we talk of bearing fruit we are talking about the fruit of the Spirit: love, joy and peace, etc. (Galatians 5:22, 23), and therefore are coming up with excuses for not bearing the character of Christ; excuses for why you don't see Christ's character in my life, and excuses for why I don't see His character in your life.

Abiding and Total Dependence

We have a tendency to come up with these varied excuses because we misunderstand the basis of fruit-bearing, thinking we are responsible for developing the fruit. So we say to ourselves, "I am going to work on patience as a fruit." "I'm going to work on love." "I'm going to love this person even if it kills me." Can you develop these fruits? It's ridiculous! Yet the Devil convinces us of this, and we become determined to do it. How many times have I talked with husbands and wives who say, "Well, I'm going to love her even if it's the last thing I ever do!" And that is totally ridiculous.

But what happens if we are abiding in the Vine? Love just comes out. If we take all, we will give all. If we give all, we'll have to take it—you can't do it without Him. No matter how much determination you muster on your own, it will still be utterly impossible to develop these fruits. What is a severed branch fit for? Burning, and it is good for nothing else. The branch lasts a minute, generates a little heat, and then it will be gone—that's the end of it, and that's exactly what Jesus intended to communicate. This illustration is so completely true and so completely simple that it's very, very difficult for us to believe it.

So the very things I want you to remember and put down in your notes from these verses of Scripture is the lesson of the branch's total and absolute dependence. The branch cannot live, it cannot exist, it cannot produce, it cannot do anything without abiding in the Vine. And it must continually abide, 24 hours a day, 365 days out of the year. It isn't a matter of abiding only on Sabbath or at the midweek service; it means abiding every day, it means abiding continually! And if the branch abides in the Vine, it cannot help but bear the fruit! That's right, it can't help but bear the fruit, for it has to; it's the natural thing and it can't help but do so. This is what righteousness by faith is really all about.

Notes:

[1] Ellen G. White, *Steps to Christ* (Mountain View, CA.: Pacific Press Publishing Association, 1956), p. 69.

[2] Ibid., p. 70.

Study Questions:

1. What is the main theme of John 15:1-8? (7)

2. What is the purpose of purging and how does it take place? (8)

3. How much can the branch do? (9)

4. What does it mean for the branch to "give and take," and what does this mean on a practical basis for the Christian? (10,11)

5. What gets between the Vine and the branch? (13)

6. To what degree does environment affect the branch's ability to bear fruit? (15)

7. What is the purpose of the branch, and how is that purpose achieved? (16)

8. What are some of the excuses made for not bearing fruit? (15)

Chapter 2

Abiding and Pruning

> *"I am the True Vine and My Father is the Husbandman. Every branch in Me that beareth not fruit He taketh away; and every branch that beareth fruit He purgeth it, that it may bring forth more fruit. Now ye are clean through the word which I have spoken unto you. Abide in Me, and I in you. As the branch cannot bear fruit of itself, except it abide in the vine; no more can ye, except ye abide in Me. I am the Vine, ye are the branches: He that abideth in Me, and I in him, the same bringeth forth much fruit: for without Me ye can do nothing. If a man abide not in Me, he is cast forth as a branch, and is withered; and men gather them, and cast them into the fire, and they are burned. If ye abide in Me, and My words abide in you, ye shall ask what ye will, and it shall be done unto you. Herein is My Father glorified, that ye bear much fruit; so shall ye be My disciples" (John 15:1-8).*

Jesus spoke these words after having celebrated the Passover and inaugurating the first Lord's Supper with His disciples. Jesus had conversed with the disciples following the meal, but eventually brought the conversation to a close and led them out into the night and proceeded towards the Garden of Gethsemane. Along the way He came to a beautiful grapevine.

A vine held great significance for the disciples, for the Jewish people had always seen themselves as the vine. Jesus wanted to correct this misconception, and so, as He stood before that moonlight-bathed vine with its clusters of grapes hanging upon it, He said, "I am the True Vine." The disciples thought they were the vine, but Jesus, using an illustration from nature as He had done on so many occasions, asserted that He was actually the True Vine and His Father was the Husbandman. "Every branch in Me that beareth not fruit He taketh away" (John 15:2).

The last time we considered this subject, we discussed the purpose of the branch, discovering that the branch's one purpose is bearing fruit. The vine supports the branch in this matter, and the branch is there as a vehicle through which the fruit is borne. Fruit-bearing is the branch's purpose!

We also discussed that it is in the area of fruit-bearing that problems exist, and that the only way the branch can bear fruit is by abiding in the vine. The branch cannot bear fruit by making any effort. The branch naturally bears the fruit as long as it does one thing: abides in the vine. It doesn't have to expend energy and effort, saying, "Well, I think I ought to have a cluster of grapes at this point." Nor does it say such a thing at some later point. It just naturally bears the fruit.

The vine does all the work. The vine sends the root and tendrils out, perhaps sending them hundreds of feet. The fine little rootlets seek nourishment and moisture in the soil, return that nourishment, convert it into rich sap, and send it up the vine to the branch. What does the branch do with the sap then? It carries the sap further. The branch is still only a vehicle, because the sap flows out into the branch and into the leaves. The leaves receive the life-giving sunshine, and the rays of light initiate a chemical process in the plant. None of this depends on the branch other than its function as the vehicle by which the sap flows. There are tremendous lessons here that need to be learned.

Now the real test of any branch is bearing fruit. If the branch fails to bear fruit, it is fit for nothing, and the Scripture says, "He taketh it away." This is interesting because in verse 2 it says, "Every branch in Me that beareth not fruit He taketh away." Did you ever wonder why the "He" is there? Who is the "He"? The Husbandman. Who is the Husbandman? The Father. God is the Husbandman, and He takes the unprofitable branch away. That should put us in our place, since a lot of us would like to do the pruning and chopping.

When you compare this with the counsel Jesus gave in Matthew 7:15, 16, and 20, you begin to get a pretty clear picture of what our role should be and what should result so far as fruit is concerned. Notice verses 15 and 16: "Beware of false prophets, who come to you in sheep's clothing, but inwardly they are ravening wolves. Ye shall know them by their fruits." Verse 20 says, "Wherefore by their fruits ye shall know them." What do we do when we recognize the fruit? We tend to make ourselves husbandmen and do the dividing ourselves! We have always had the tendency to ask, "Lord shall we take out the weeds?" Notice how Jesus responded in His day: "Let them grow until the harvest." Who then must do the dividing, the separating, and the weeding? Only the Husbandman, because weeding is God's business, not ours, and I praise His name for that. And, you know, even though fruit isn't all that easy to detect by human vision—which is why it isn't safe for humans to do the weeding—God still says we will know them by their fruits.

Accordingly, when prophets claim to be something, we can "know them by their fruits." Why? Because we can always check the fruit by the Word. Through God's Word we can detect the presence of fruit. But when we have recognized fruit, all we have done—and we must remember this—is increased our knowledge. But even then, it is not for us to pass judgment, for judgment is left entirely to God. But God has given us a way to detect the presence of fruit. So, "by their fruits" is the guideline we have been given. Reading further, it says, "Every branch that beareth not fruit He taketh away."

A Single Purpose

Andrew Murray,[3] states in his book, *The Mystery of the True Vine*:

> *"Let us specially beware of one great mistake. Many Christians think their own salvation is the first thing; their temporal life and prosperity, with the care of their family the second; and what of time and interest is left may be devoted to fruit-bearing, to the saving of men. No wonder that in most cases very little time or interest can be found. No, Christian, the one object with which you have been made a member of God's body is that the Head may have you carry out His saving work. The one object God had in making you a branch is that Christ may through you bring life to men. Your personal salvation, your business and care for your family, are entirely subordinate to this."*[4]

I am sure you didn't get this. Let me repeat part of it, "The one object God had in making you a branch is that Christ may through you bring life to men." God says, "I am the Vine, ye are the branches," and His one object for you is to make you a branch through which life can be imparted to men. Through what? The fruit! The fruit is what nourishes anyone who comes to the vine. Isn't that true? And if we are the branches, we are to bear fruit and thus supply the food through which the world is to know the Lord Jesus.

"The one object God (has) in making you a branch is that Christ may through you bring life to men." Might this be the reason we read that God is waiting for His people to perfectly reflect His image? Why? Because men and women can only feed on what they really see, and are only attracted to come to Christ on the basis of what they see as well. "The one object God (has) in making you a branch is that Christ may through you bring life to men. Your personal salvation . . ."—this is where we fall off the track—"Your personal salvation, your business and care for your family, are entirely subordinate to this one thing."

That's a broad statement. It is so easy for me to first care for myself, my family, and children. Taking care of my family causes me to feel like I have accomplished something noble and good, because any man who looks after his family is thought of as a very fine person—and that is great and there's nothing wrong with that. But our first and primary purpose for existence is not caring for our families. What is our first and primary purpose? Bearing fruit.

You see, our first obligation to God is fruit-bearing, not our salvation. If my relationship with God is wholly about salvation, then my relationship with Him is selfish. But if I have a relationship with God in order to abide in the Vine and am a faithful, fruit-bearing branch, then I am fulfilling the purpose for which God created me, as expressed in John 15:5: "I am the Vine, ye are the branches." It doesn't mean the family will be ignored, however, for the family will be cared for, and will be the first to benefit from this abiding.

Now notice that your first aim in life, your first aim every day, should be to know how Christ desires to carry out His purposes in you—that's the very first aim. Did you ever read that Christ's first work every morning was seeking direction from His Heavenly Father as to what He was to do that day? Our first work should be the same: receiving our instructions fresh every morning.

Fruitful Branches

Now notice what Andrew Murray says next:

> *"Let us begin to think as God thinks. Let us accept Christ's teaching and respond to it. The one object of my being a branch, the one mark of my being a true branch, the one condition of my*

abiding and growing strong, is that I bear the fruit of the heavenly Vine for dying men to eat and live. The one thing of which I can have the most perfect assurance is that, with Christ as my Vine, and the Father as my Husbandman, I can indeed be a fruitful branch."[5]

No one needs to feel they cannot be a fruitful branch. Every person can be a fruitful branch! Jesus says that if a branch is not bearing fruit, The husbandman cuts it off. But the Husbandman cuts it off in His Own time and in His Own way—that's His business, not ours. But every branch that is bearing fruit, He purges it. So the fruit-bearing becomes the real problem in most people's thinking because we are subject to deception and Satan has caused us to misunderstand what fruit-bearing really is. But here Jesus says that every branch that beareth fruit, He purgeth it, that it may bring forth more fruit.

A Dangerous Complacency

Accordingly, the real danger in any Christian life, and I mean the very real and serious danger in any Christian life, is complacency. Do you believe that? Perhaps you ask, "What do you mean using the word complacency?" Revelation 3:14-18 provides the answer in the message to the church in Laodicea. What was the problem there? Lukewarmness. The problem of lukewarmness has faced the church throughout history, but is particularly true of today's church, which also happens to be the last church.

"And unto the angel of the church of the Laodiceans write; These things saith the Amen, the faithful and True Witness, the Beginning of the creation of God; I know thy works, that thou art neither cold nor hot: I would thou wert cold or hot. So then because thou art lukewarm, and neither cold nor hot, I will spew thee out of My mouth. Because thou sayest, I am rich, and increased with goods, and have need of nothing; and knowest not that thou art wretched, and miserable, and poor, and blind, and naked: I counsel thee to buy of Me gold tried in the fire, that thou mayest be rich; and white raiment, that thou mayest be clothed, and that the shame of thy nakedness do not appear; and anoint thine eyes with eyesalve, that thou mayest see" (Revelation 3:14-18).

The problem that comes to every Christian along the way is not a *lack* of fruit-bearing. Rather, when he finds himself feeling that he has borne a little fruit, felt a little of the love of God and the joy of salvation, has enjoyed a little experience and is feeling elevated about the whole thing, he settles down and *remembers that experience* the rest of his life. He lives on it, and talks about it, but doesn't go any further. And he accordingly misses the "more fruit" element of being the branch. But the capacity of the branch is tremendous, and the Husbandman comes along and begins to prune the branch in order to produce more fruit.

Pruning and Fruit-bearing

So, what is it that produces "more fruit"? And who is it that produces "more fruit"? The pruning or purging process is intended to do one thing: draw us into a closer relationship to God, that we might be a more efficient vehicle through which the fruit is revealed—that's the purpose.

The thing we need to settle, then, is who does this pruning, and how does the pruning process really take place?

Notice the following quotation that speaks of our possible union with Christ, which in the parable is described as the relationship between the branch and the Vine.

> *"A union with Christ by living faith is enduring; every other union must perish. Christ first chose us, paying an infinite price for our redemption; and the true believer chooses Christ as first, and last, and best in everything. But this union costs us something. It is a relation of utter dependence, to be entered into by a proud being."*[6]

We have to stop right here. "It is a relationship of utter dependence, to be entered into by a proud being." How is pride affected? We are proud! We all have proud, egocentric natures, and the only way we can be free from this pride is to recognize the purpose of the branch. There is only one source of strength for the branch. What is that source? The Vine. The Vine is our Source of strength, our only Source of strength. But do we look to the Source? No! We look everywhere else. We go to Aunt Jenny and we go to Uncle Tom. We go everywhere. We read everything. We try anything and everything to find this strength, except going to the Vine to find it. Why? Because we don't like the Vine's solution: drinking deeper of the blood of Jesus Christ.

The branch doesn't support the Vine, does it? Absolutely not! The branch continually receives from the vine—that's the branch's purpose, and it is simply the vehicle. Our relationship with God is to function the same way. That's why God said, ". . . to be entered into by a proud being." Why? Because it is a humbling process. It is humbling to realize we can do nothing by ourselves; it is humbling to realize that a branch cut off from the Vine is only fit to be gathered and burned, according to verse six.

Now we read, "All who form this union must feel their need of the atoning blood of Christ."[7] That's the lifeblood. The branch must feel its need of the life-giving flow of sap, which is the atoning blood of Christ. If the death, burial, and resurrection of Christ are not a reality to you and me, if the atonement paid on Calvary's cross is not a reality; if these are not real and central points in our thinking, our religion is vain, and we are tied to the wrong vine. Remember, Christ is the Vine, and when we receive strength from the Vine, we receive it from Christ.

Notice as well that Christ received the wound by which we have been grafted in. Paul speaks of the grafting process in Romans 11:17, where he speaks of our having been grafted into the Vine. Now before a graft can be made in any plant, what has to happen to the plant? It has to be wounded. A cut has to be made that severely wounds the stalk, and this cut opens the wound into which the graft is inserted. Thus, the graft obtains its life as a result of the wound.

The strength of your life and mine comes from the atonement—it comes from no other place. Hiding in the atonement is His power. It isn't because Jesus Christ was the Creator, as great and marvelous as that was; nor is it because He demonstrated miraculous power in calling forth the dead, which was also wonderful and thrilling. The one thing that gives me life is that Jesus as God was willing to die—was wounded—enabling me to be grafted in and to receive life. In spite of that, we go along complacently thinking that life comes as a result of doing something good. That's ridiculous! The only source of life is to be found in partaking of that sap, which is none other than the blood of Jesus Christ. There is no other source of life! If we don't receive it there, we simply don't have it.

Reading on, "They must have a change of heart."[8] Who? The branch. The branch, which was cut off from its own stock and put into the True Vine to receive the new heart, is going to receive a new source of life and will have a new kind of fruit as it draws nourishment from the Vine.

The branch is going to have a new kind of experience—termed a new heart—because the heart of Jesus Christ is now supplying the life flow to that branch.

Pruning and Submission

Next, our passage says, "They must submit their own will to the will of God."[9] Here is where troubles begin. "They must submit their own will to the will of God. There will be a struggle with outward and internal obstacles. There must be a painful work of detachment as well as a work of attachment." What must we be detached from? Pride—that's the very first thing you see. Remember, we read about this relationship as being, "entered into by a proud being," and so we're cut off from that old source of pride, cut off from the stalk from which pride grew. And to pride, we can add, "selfishness, vanity, worldliness—sin in all its forms—must be overcome. . . ."[10]

There is only one way to overcome all of this, and that is to be cut off from it. You must cut off the life source of pride, selfishness, and sin in all of its forms—which is actually the world. So we must be cut off from our love of the world. That's why the Bible says that if we love the world, the love of the Father is not in us. So we cannot compromise. We cannot bring the world and the Lord Jesus Christ together; we cannot blend them, for they are diametrically opposed. Any person who thinks the world can be held with one hand and the Lord Jesus Christ with the other hand, is fooling themselves and attempting an utter impossibility.

Reading further, "Pride, selfishness, vanity, worldliness—sin in all its forms—must be overcome, if we would enter into a union with Christ. The reason why many find the Christian life so deplorably hard, why they are so fickle . . ."—what does the word fickle mean? Changeable, unstable, saying one thing but doing another—"The reason . . ."—I like statements that get right to the "this is it" nitty-gritty—"The reason why many find the Christian life so deplorably hard, why they are so fickle, so variable, is that they try to attach themselves to Christ without first detaching themselves from their cherished idols."[11]

The Branch's Helplessness

The problem here is manifested in the first part of the sentence, where it speaks of our attempt to attach ourselves to Christ. When the branch is attached to the Vine, who does the attaching? The Husbandman. The problem comes when I think I can attach myself to the Lord Jesus Christ and I want to do it my own way. And of course when I attach myself to the Vine my own way, I certainly don't take the difficult, painstaking way of going through the grafting process. Why? Because not only does the parent stalk have to be wounded, but if I'm going to be grafted in, I have to be severely pruned—wounded—too.

They don't take a gigantic branch which has borne all kinds of fruit and just graft it in. No, they prune that branch down; they trim it, cut it and fit it into the wound; then they bind it into the wound of the parent stalk. As a result, the branch begins to receive entirely new nourishment. Now if I did this myself, I would say, "Lord, let's just You and I walk together. I'll need Your help a little along the way. I really am sincere and I think I can make it, but I will probably need Your help a little bit." Unfortunately, this is the Christian philosophy of many, many people. "Just stay close by, Lord, because whenever I stumble and get into difficulty I'll need Your help.

Jesus said, "Without Me ye can do nothing." And so, as Jesus was talking to His disciples that last evening, He was trying to help them understand their helplessness. Do you understand your helplessness? Do you? This is *the* important question, and many do sense it, since they talk to me about their helplessness. We must all feel our utter dependence upon God. What does the word "utter" mean? Extreme; it means our extreme dependence upon God.

Unconditional Surrender

Notice this statement, "Until the heart is surrendered unconditionally to God, the human agent is not abiding in the True Vine . . ."[12] Let me repeat that, "Until the heart is surrendered unconditionally . . ." What does it mean to surrender unconditionally? It means to surrender without any reservations. "Until the heart is surrendered unconditionally to God, the human agent is not abiding in the True Vine, and cannot flourish in the Vine and bear rich clusters of fruit." There is only one way the human agent can do this, and that is by unconditionally surrendering to the Vine.

Let's think about this process for a moment. The fruit-bearing branch first receives purging. What is purging? It is when the branch is pruned. What do you think God uses for His pruning or purging process? Some people suggest that God uses trials. If that is the case, it would seem that some people are not being pruned very much. Some might suggest that the "easy road" is indicative of the pruning process or the lack thereof in the lives of some individuals.

Pruning and God's Word

It is interesting that many Christians believe God uses the trials and tribulations that are allowed to come our way in the course of the pruning process. Being perfectly honest, most of us would agree. It may surprise you, then, to know that John 15:3 suggests something quite different. Before Jesus told His disciples about the necessity of abiding, He said, "Now ye are clean through the word which I have spoken unto you." I am completely convinced that the Word of God, and the Word of God *alone*, is the knife that does the pruning—I am absolutely satisfied with this.

We may have trials and tribulations along the way, but these don't really bother us. *The thing that bothers us about trials and tribulations is the solution the Word gives for them.* Do you believe that? Are you following me? You see, problems come our way, we search for the solution in the Word of God, and find a clear solution. Generally that solution is "believe on Me," "abide in Me," "trust Me." We don't like that solution because it's much easier to get along with ourselves if we do something. But where is our only source of strength? The Bible and what it reveals about Jesus Christ! This is the source of strength, but we look for it everywhere else. We go to Aunt Jenny and Uncle Tom. We go everywhere, we read everything, we try every possibility, to get this strength, except receiving it from the Vine. Why? Because we don't like the Vine's solution: drink deeper of the blood of Jesus Christ.

The Bible reveals only one thing: Jesus Christ, and Him crucified. From Genesis to Revelation one story is repeated over and over again in multitudinous ways, and that is the life and vicarious death of Jesus Christ for you and me—that's the only story told in the Bible, and that story forms your life and mine. But it's not appealing because the branch cannot do anything except simply appreciate it, rest in it and trust completely in it—that's all, and it's not very thrilling or glamorous; and it's not something you beat drums over. You simply rest and believe in it.

Pruning and Feelings

Jesus knew how important understanding this would be, and gave the disciples this insight just before they entered into the most catastrophic experience they could possibly enter into. Just a few hours later they would face the most depressing and awful event of their lives. Just a few hours from then Jesus would die, and they would be hanging their heads and saying, "We trusted that it had been He that would have delivered Israel." And Jesus warned, unless you are abiding in the Vine when this happens, your feelings will overcome you. If, however, you drink deeply of the blood of Jesus Christ the Vine, your feelings will be overcome; you won't be subject to them.

It is tragic that we find it so hard to learn that instead of our feelings governing us, we are to govern our feelings. Why? Because it is only when we no longer abide in Christ that our feelings can really touch us. And I don't care whether it's you or anyone else, anytime my feelings are hurt—and my feelings are just like yours—anytime my feelings are hurt or affected in any way, it is because I am not receiving my joy and strength—that which is the fruit of the Spirit—from the Vine. I am instead trying to receive them from an outside source. If I receive them from Christ, does it matter what happens to me? If He is the Source of my joy and strength, does it matter what happens to me from the outside? That's why Paul wrote so eloquently, "Though I have gone through shipwreck, starvation . . ." and ended the whole thing mentioning, "the care of the churches," none of these things bothers me (2 Corinthians 11:25-28). Not one of these experiences bothered Paul because he had found the Source of his life. That Source has to be the Vine, and that's what we're talking about.

If we learn to abide in the Vine, the stormy tempests that come along won't buffet us, regardless of their source. But tell me: When did you last find yourself depressed on account of your feelings? When did you last find yourself motivated by feelings? When did you last find yourself doing something because you *felt* a particular way? We are such slaves to feelings, and Satan takes advantage of them to get at us. And there is no way to get rid of them except by abiding in the Vine—that's the only way. Abiding in the Vine, feelings depart.

Jesus said, "Now ye are clean through the word" (John 15:3). If you get the full meaning of this, you will find Jesus was really saying, "Now ye are clean through belief in the word which I have spoken unto you." The disciples didn't believe it at that moment, but a few hours later, they began to see. And a few days later, they saw even more! Things looked different, and they realized Jesus knew what He had been talking about. And these men who had been struggling with the vacillating feelings that we've been studying about, became strong and stalwart; in fact, as strong as can be. Peter, who vacillated between being hot one minute and cold the next, became a stalwart for God. Why? Because he learned to abide in the Lord; because he learned to wait on the Lord; because he learned to trust in the Lord; because he learned to believe on the Lord.

May God bless you as you learn to abide in the Vine.

Notes:

[3] Andrew Murray wrote some very interesting and worthwhile material. Among his books are *The Mystery of the True Vine* and *Abiding in Christ*.

[4] Andrew Murray, *The Mystery of the True Vine* (London: Nisbet, 1898), p. 33.

[5] Ibid.

[6] Ellen G. White, *Messages to Young People* (Nashville, TN: Southern Publishing Association, 1930), p. 118

[7] Ibid.

[8] Ibid.

[9] Ibid.

[10] Ibid.

[11] Ibid.

[12] Ellen G. White, *Sons and Daughters of God* (Hagerstown, MD: Review and Herald, 1955), p. 288

Study Questions:

1. What is the one object for which God made us branches? (22)

2. In what way is complacency dangerous in the Christian life? (23-24)

3. What is the purpose of pruning and what does the pruning? (24,28)

4. What kind of surrender is necessary to abide in the Vine? (27)

5. What is the solution to the "feeling" problem? (29)

Chapter 3

Abiding and Daily Living

Let's briefly review what we have studied so far.

We have been considering the precious counsel that Jesus gave His disciples just before He went to His death. This was in effect His last will and testament, and He gave it after leaving the upper room and before He entered the Garden of Gethsemane. He couldn't have had much time to talk with them, at most a couple of hours.

Coming upon a beautiful vine that was shimmering in the moonlight, and which the Jews took as an apt symbol of themselves as a people and nation, Jesus surprised the disciples by saying, "I am the True Vine." It must have been hard to hear and shocking that the very Person the Jewish people were rejecting was identifying Himself as the True Vine.

We find the conversation recorded in John 15. Jesus first pointed out that He was the True Vine and His Father was the Husbandman. In verse two, He told the disciples that unfruitful branches would be taken away, but branches bearing fruit would be purged that they might bear more fruit.

In verse three, He revealed that cleansing would come by way of His word: "Ye are clean through the word that I have spoken unto you." In studying this verse, we learned that cleansing only comes through the Word of God. We also learned that the Word revealed from Genesis to Revelation points to one thing, and that is Christ! Jesus said, "You search the Scriptures, for in them ye think ye have eternal life, and they are they which testify of Me" (John 5:39).

Let's read John 15: 4 and 5.

> *"Abide in Me, and I in you. As the branch cannot bear fruit of itself except it abide in the vine, no more can ye, except ye abide in Me. I am the Vine, ye are the branches: He that abideth in Me, and I in him, the same bringeth forth much fruit: for without Me ye can do nothing."*

Purging: A Necessary Continuing Process

To appreciate these verses, we need to review the pruning or purging that is done on a vine. Anyone who has worked in a vineyard knows what I am referring to. We used to have a vineyard, and discovered that going through and pruning all the branches was a big job.

The spiritual pruning we are learning about is also a big job. To really understand, we need to not only know "what" does the pruning, but also "who" does the pruning.

Regarding the "what" does the pruning" question, Jesus was talking about the Word. But accepting that the Word does the pruning isn't easy. Why? Because we are disinclined to accept God's counsel! You see, when the Bible identifies something that needs pruning, we usually argue against it, preferring to rationalize, saying, "I think it is all right for the Smiths, but I'm not sure it is right for the Joneses." Yet, though we prefer to apply the counsel to others, the Bible speaks directly to us for the purpose of bringing conviction and correction, which is precisely what we need.

Pruning makes it possible for us to bear more fruit. The only way to produce more fruit is through the learning process, where the things learned are personally applied. Merely knowing the Scriptures is inadequate and won't help us. The Word only becomes profitable when the learning is applied, and fruit will be borne as a result.

Fruit-bearing isn't about getting lots of people to surrender their lives to the Lord Jesus Christ. No, fruit-bearing is rather what Paul talked about in the book of Galatians when he said the fruit of the Spirit is love, joy, peace, long-suffering, gentleness, goodness, faith, meekness, and temperance (Galatians 5:22). All of these are the fruit—Paul uses the singular form in this instance—of the Spirit, because the Christian life reflects all of them, and it is God's plan that there be abundant fruit.

Understanding that the Word does the cleansing or pruning, we need to also consider "Who" does the pruning that brings about the more abundant fruit?

It is the Vine that causes the fruit to be produced. But though the Vine produces fruit, the branch can't bear anything unless it abides in the Vine and receives its nourishment from the Vine, which results in the branch becoming a channel through which fruit is produced. This has been God's purpose for us from the beginning.

Reciprocal Abiding

But there are problems connected with this, for at the same time that it speaks of Christ being the Vine and our needing to abide in the Vine, it also speaks of Christ abiding in the branch, which makes it essential that we keep reading to where it says, "Abide in Me," and then "I abide in you" (John 15:4). It's a two-way street.

Many individuals have attached themselves to the church thinking they have attached themselves to the Lord Jesus Christ. They feel they have obtained the security or insurance they need by attaching themselves to the organization. But this kind of attaching has nothing to do with salvation or genuine security. Security only comes as we not only abide in Him, but as He also abides in us—that's the real source of security!

So while Jesus makes it clear in these verses that He is the One who produces the ever increasing fruit in our lives, while we abide in Him, that fruit is the result of His abiding in us.

Fruit-bearing and Commandment-keeping

How do we compare these verses in John 15 with the verses in Revelation 22:14, where Jesus said, "Blessed are they that do His commandments, that they may have right to the tree of life, and may enter in through the gates into the city"? That's been a strong and encouraging text to many church members, and has buoyed up their spirits for a long time. Modern translations render these words, "Blessed are they that wash their robes;" which is different and doesn't sit well with some people, but is part of the ancient manuscripts; and we need to accept their rendering too—in fact, it is the same thing.

How would you compare and explain these two verses of Scripture? What was being said? Jesus said, "Without Me, ye can do nothing" (John 15: 5). He also said, "Abide in Me, and I in you. As the branch cannot bear fruit of itself, except it abide in the vine; no more can ye, except ye abide in Me" (John 15:4). In Revelation 22:14 we find, "Blessed are they that do His commandments, that they may have right to the tree of life." How do we integrate these two? Are they a paradox? Are they contradictory? Can they be harmonized? How can they be harmonized?

Now in and of ourselves, it is utterly impossible for us to keep the commandments of God; anyone who thinks he can is fooling himself;

and it is ridiculous to try the impossible! The Jews were a good example of this, for at the same time that they were teaching the law they were seeking to kill Him. Though they believed the law that said "Thou shalt not kill," they were still plotting to take His life even at that very moment. Such is the outcome of man's ridiculous reasoning when he tries to carry out divine principles on his own. Divine principles can only be carried out as the Holy Spirit lives and guides and interprets in our experience that which is right and true.

Notice Mark 12:29-31, where it states:

> "Jesus answered him, *'The first of all the commandments is, Hear O Israel; The Lord our God is one Lord: and thou shalt love the Lord thy God with all thy heart, and with all thy soul, and with all thy mind, and with all thy strength: this is the first commandment.'*"

Do you see that this is the first commandment of the ten, in expanded form? Being honest, are you able to keep that commandment? Of course not! It is utterly impossible. Only as the Holy Spirit does this in and through you is it possible; you simply can't. But you can choose to do it; you can set your will to do it. That is why the Christian life is lived totally in the "will," and not in the "way." Now that doesn't mean that the "way" does not come into harmony with the "will," but the human does not direct the "way." Rather the human directs the "will," and the "way" becomes directed by the Holy Spirit. But that is precisely where we fall down, for we try to do God's part, and want God to do our part.

Putting God in the Driver's Seat

Our part is to choose to enter God's plan in any and all circumstances. But it is so easy to take ourselves out of God's plan and place ourselves—as one person put it—in the driver's seat when any disturbing factors come along. It is interesting that God so easily responds to our desire to take over the wheel again; He doesn't put up a fight. Even though He is "driving" and directing our lives, anytime we want to take over, He simply moves out of the way. Does He say, "No, stop, think about what you are doing. Listen to Me. I'm directing the course and getting along fine. If you take over you're going to end up in the ditch"? No, He simply moves over, allows me to take over the driving, and I eventually find myself in the ditch. And it happens all the time.

Perhaps you have never been in the ditch. If you have, however, it always resulted from your taking over the driver's seat—that's what happens in my life, for whenever I take over, I find myself in the ditch, I end up having to call for service, and the Lord comes and gets me out. That's the routine, and it happens time and time again until we finally recognize our inability to control or guide ourselves.

Loving God Supremely
Loving Our Neighbor as Ourself

In John 15:12 Jesus said, "This is My commandment, That ye love one another, as I have loved you." Now what was the first commandment? "Thou shalt love the Lord thy God with all thy heart, with all thy soul, and with all thy mind, and with all thy strength." How much is left? Not much! So the first commandment is "love to God." The second commandment is "Thou shalt love thy neighbor as thyself."

It is utterly impossible to put this second commandment into words, even in the Bible, because though the Bible is composed of divinely inspired human words, they are still inadequate, since they are of human origin and best suited to describe human things. When attempting to grasp the full meaning of the first commandment "Thou shalt love the Lord thy God with all thy heart, with all thy soul, and with all thy mind, and with all thy strength," when we try to comprehend everything that is intended, we acknowledge our human inability to fully understand. So God sent Jesus to this planet to give us a living demonstration of the love that is the outworking of this commandment.

In simple terms Jesus said, "Thou shalt love thy neighbor as thyself." Jesus expressed the same idea with other words when He said, "That ye love one another, as I have loved you" (John 13:34; 15:12). How do I love my neighbor as myself? I love my neighbor as myself in the same way Jesus loved me. Does that make it any easier to understand? If it doesn't, all I have to do is return to the Scriptures and study the life of Christ, for there in His life are exemplified all the teachings of Scripture. Every doctrine, every teaching, every single experience of life, is wrapped up in Christ, and nothing is missing. If I want to find answers for life's problems, I go to the Scriptures. Jesus said, "You search the Scriptures; for in them ye think ye have eternal life: and they are they which testify of Me" (John 5:39).

Jesus' life, Jesus' whole purpose—His work for mankind through the plan of redemption—was exemplified in the Old Testament shadows of the sacrificial system; it was all there! He was the Lamb; He was the Offering. Every part of that service depicted Christ's life, but very few people understood in His day. In our day, not only can we find this purpose depicted in the shadows of the sacrificial system in the Old Testament, but we can find it also exemplified and lived out in Christ's life.

The Essential Task

Reading John 15:4, 5 again,

> *"Abide in Me, and I in you. As the branch cannot bear fruit of itself, except it abide in the vine, no more can ye, except ye abide in Me. I am the Vine, ye are the branches. He that abideth in Me, and I in him, the same bringeth forth much fruit: for without Me ye can do nothing."*

So what is the real purpose and task of the branch? More times than not, most people will suggest bearing fruit and abiding. Regarding bearing fruit, we tend to think about the end result and the production of fruit. We are so anxious for end results. Few people are naturally patient. Do you know many patient people? I've yet to meet a person who was naturally patient by birth. Genuine human patience is the result of the Lord Jesus coming into the human heart. People can endure things, but to be naturally patient and wait on the Lord is something else!

Most of us want to get in and do things for ourselves, whatever the situation may be; we are not willing to wait for the Lord. The problem that comes with being a branch and bearing fruit, so far as the end result is concerned, is that you can't do anything about it; all you can do is stay hooked to the Vine. What can you do about bearing fruit? Can you get more leaves? Can you produce fruit on your own? Is there anything else you can do? Nothing! You only have one task: Abide!

Abiding, putting yourself *into* God's Vine, is something you can do. You can also move into the driver's seat and take yourself *out of* God's Vine any time you want to, and God won't put up any fuss about it. He doesn't object. He just moves over and lets you see what happens. So you can take yourself out of the Vine anytime you want to, and many of us have been in and out hundreds of times.

Being Cut Off From the Source

To find the real answer to this abiding and fruit-bearing business, we simply need to look at it from the reverse side and ask, "Which areas is Satan most actively working in?" Does he work on you relative to abiding and keeping yourself in Christ, or does he work on you relative to producing fruit? His goal is to break your contact with God. He knows fruit-bearing will take care of itself. When he gets you to concentrate on the fruit, he is trying to produce a fruit through you that God didn't intend, as well as causing you to also cease abiding in the Vine and abide instead in self. Instead of producing the fruit God wants you to bear, you produce self-righteousness. The only way to produce the fruit of righteousness—what Paul called the fruit of the Spirit—is by abiding in the Vine; otherwise you produce self-righteousness, and none of us is exempt. You may not think so, but it is true nevertheless.

So Satan focuses on the fruit, but his object is to cut us off from the Source. This is clearly portrayed in Scripture, where Jesus spoke of the people who would approach Him at the time of His Second Coming, saying, "Lord, we don't deserve the treatment You're giving us because we were with You all the way. We even performed many miracles in Your power. We cast out devils, we healed the sick, and we performed miracle after miracle in Your name." But the Master's words are going to be, "Depart from me, ye workers of iniquity; I never knew you" (Matthew 7: 22, 23).

Abiding, Yet Not Abiding

Apparently it is possible to abide in the Vine, and yet *not* abide in the Vine, which suggests that we may be using the wrong term and need to establish some definitions.

> *"If a man abide not in Me, he is cast forth as a branch, and is withered; and men gather them, and cast them into the fire, and they are burned"* John 15:6.

This verse depicts a time in the future when the bundles—branches that were cut off—will be gathered and burned in the final end. This indicates that it is possible to remain in the Vine and yet not abide.

I went to Webster's dictionary to find the various definitions of "abiding." I was shocked by what I discovered, and wrote down four different definitions: "to endure without yielding," "to bear patiently," " to accept without objection," and "to remain stable." We could have a good discussion on any of these, but I think we can readily agree that abiding includes the possibility of yeilding while being in the Vine, or fail to endure.

Jesus referred to yielding individuals who are blown about by every wind of doctrine, and yet feel they are connected to the Vine. They think they are abiding; they trust that they are abiding. If this were not possible, we wouldn't have individuals coming and saying, "Lord, You treated me wrong! I was sincere in this, but I was fooled. I couldn't tell I was fooled, but I was. I thought for sure that I was abiding in the Vine." If this matter of "abiding, yet not abiding" were not possible, there wouldn't be the group that comes and says, "Lord, You treated me wrong. I don't deserve this at all. I deserve better treatment because I did all of those things in Your name." So abiding isn't a matter of feelings; it isn't a matter of feeling good, bad, or indifferent.

Abiding and God's Word

To understand this we need to go back to our discussions of purging. What is it that purges? The Word of God. If my life doesn't harmonize with the Word all the way through, I am fooling myself. We can internally fool ourselves by being overly influenced by positive or negative feelings; in the one case feeling purging is unneccessary, or in the second case feeling the pain and consequences that might come with purging, and therefore have an unpurged and unfruitful branch that may eventually be cut off. But we also recognize that the cutting off doesn't occur until the burning takes place.

If I have accepted the Lord Jesus Christ, my name can be blotted out only when probation's door closes. That will also be the time when the purging takes place. Does God write my name on His list today, only to take it back off tomorrow? Isn't it the same with the "tare"? I am told, "Let both grow together (the wheat and the tare) until the harvest" (Matthew 13:30). When is this? Should I be purging it out now? No! Jesus said to let it grow.

Security doesn't come by way of feelings, nor does it come by way of having my name on the church books. It isn't how I feel that counts; rather it is how the Word has done its work in my life that matters, to what degree I have allowed the Word to do its purging work. It is this that determines whether I am abiding in the Vine or not. The branch that refuses the purging is not going to bear fruit, even though it may bear a little fruit—at least bearing what seems like fruit—on its own. But is it real fruit? No!

Transmitting the Character of Christ

What, then, is the fruit? The fruit is simply the transmission of the character of Jesus Christ to the human body. What we are referring to is sanctification. Justification is the acceptance of God's plan of salvation whereby He atones for me. It is God's gift on Calvary. In accepting this gift, I am justified. But if justification is my title to Heaven, my fitness for Heaven depends on the purging; and the purging is about sanctification, not justification. Justification always comes first; sanctification also begins immediately at the time of justification, but the process lasts a lifetime. How long does purging go on? All the time! What is the purpose of purging? Take us deeper and deeper into the character of Jesus, that His character might be imparted to us. So when Christ takes a look at the branch that is bearing lots of nice fruit, He notices that there is a bit here and there that needs to be trimmed off, and He trims it. It is the ongoing work of sanctification that keeps justifcation current.

We must remember that knowledge of the Scriptures does not build men. The Scriptures only lead men to Jesus, who builds men —that's the purpose of the Scriptures. Prophecy, teachings, beliefs, everything you learn without Jesus is worthless.

The branch doesn't worry about fruit-bearing, does it? But the Devil tries to get you worrying about bearing fruit, and the more you worry about bearing fruit, the less fruit you will bear. Your job and mine as branches is to abide in the Vine. The branch cannot help but bear fruit if it is abiding in the Vine. It will happen!

Accepting The Purging

But the purging only goes on as the branch accepts the purging. If the branch refuses to be purged, there is nothing that can be done to help it. If you will not accept the purging brought about by the Scriptures to correct your life and bring it into harmony with the teachings of those

Scriptures, there is nothing that can be done. You will be deceived and will continue to be deceived the rest of your life.

Abiding in the Vine does not force the branch to unwillingly bear fruit. The fruit appears because the branch has become a channel, and has subjected itself—we might say permitted itself—to be pruned or purged in order to bear more fruit. Unfortunately, we sometimes create temptations for ourselves and get ahead of the Lord, creating situations and problems God never intended us to face. But if we are abiding in the Vine, we won't have to worry about these problems, since He will solve them through the abiding process in us. I'm not the one making decisions, then, for the purging process works as I permit myself to be subjected to it. That purging process is the Bible cutting out habits from my life and cutting me away from the world. Then it becomes a matter of judging all temptations and activities that Satan brings through the lens of God's Word, and not through my wisdom.

Trusting God through this process becomes a pleasure. Why? Because you will be pleased with the transformation that occurs through the pruning process. It isn't a pleasure if the pruning process isn't taking place.

Finally, do you recall the statement quoted earlier, where it talks about why so many people find the Christian life so deplorably hard?

> *"The reason why many find the Christian life so deplorably hard, why they are so fickle, so variable, is, they try to attach themselves to Christ without detaching themselves from . . . cherished idols."*[13]

This detaching is what makes the difference. If I am not detached, the detaching takes place through the purging or pruning process. And if this pruning process detaches me from the world, then the bearing of the fruit is a joy and a pleasure.

Gladly Accepting

Now if I find it hard to accept the pruning process, I may have to follow the same course that one person followed when God convicted her that meat was not the best food. Initially she ignored the counsel, and continued eating meat. This went on for quite some time, and in fact God brought the same message to her three or four times. Eventually she was convicted that meat was to be given up and determined to get rid of it from her diet. She decided she was going to stop eating meat come what may, and told the cook to only serve vegetables and fruit. Coming to the table for the first time she was repulsed by seeing only vegetables and fruit, and her stomach became upset—so much so that she couldn't eat. So she left the table and went about her business. The next time she came to the table the same thing happened again. Again she was repulsed and her stomach rebelled. "You can wait stomach until you will gladly accept this," she said, and again turned back to other duties. This went on for three days, until she was finally so hungry that she gladly ate the food that was served. So we see that she willingly accepted God's purging in spite of the hardship of temporarily going without food. Not only did she accept the purging, she accepted it joyfully—gladly! It was anything but easy, but it worked, and we can follow this same purging process with any of our besetting habits.

Doing My Part

Notice, however, what normally happens: We come to recognize an evil in our lives, come under conviction about it, and accept God's correcting; but instead of letting God continue dealing with it, we take it back into our own hands to manage, and fall back into temptation again. How did the person respond? "You can wait until you will accept that food gladly;" and victory was eventually gained. When we turn away until it becomes a joy to obey God in whatever area He is bringing conviction, we too will gain the victory.

We find the following instructive quotation in W.W. Prescott's book, *Victory in Christ*[14]:

> *"For a long time I tried to gain the victory over sin, but I failed. I have since learned the reason. Instead of doing the part which God expects me to do*—which we have learned is abiding in the Vine, to use the imagery and language we have been utilizing in these discussions—*and which I can do, I was trying to do God's part, which He does not expect me to do, and which I cannot do. Primarily, my part is not to win the victory—and produce the fruit—but to receive the victory*—receive the Holy Spirit and let Him produce the fruit—*which has already been won for me by Jesus Christ"*—when He took the place of Adam and day by day developed the character which Adam failed to acquire. Jesus won the victory; He won the victory over Satan and sin.

Jesus wants to give us His victory, but He's having an awful time getting us to accept it. Why? Because we are unwilling to do our part, which is abiding in Him, and allowing Him to accomplish the pruning, which will result in the development of His character in us. It doesn't sound too difficult, but it is, because as He grafts us into the Vine, and we begin growing, little sprouts have a way of appearing that look suspiciously like the old life. He determines these need to be cut off and proceeds, but we find the cutting exceedingly painful, object to it, which results in His relenting and responding, "I'm not going to continue pruning if you don't allow Me." But the outcome is a turning away, the impeding of His life being lived out in us, and the reemergence of the old life; He can only live in us if we permit Him to!

Striving and Bearing Fruit

"'But,' you will ask, 'does not the Bible speak about soldiers, and warfare, and a fight?' Yes, it certainly does. 'Are we not told that we must strive to enter in?' We surely are. 'Well, what then?' Only this, that we should be sure for what we are fighting, and for what we are to strive,"[15]—which is to abide in the Vine!

We are not to worry about the fruit, which is receiving God's character. When God's people perfectly reflect His character, Jesus will come to claim them as His own. There is only one thing God is waiting for, and that is for the perfection of the fruit which He imparts to the human body, the human mind, and the human person, through the process of sanctification—which is simply the imparting of His character to us. Sanctification is His gift, just as justification is His gift; both are gifts from first to last.

We need to also recognize that hindering factors can prevent us from enjoying these gifts. Did you ever try to give someone something, but were deterred due to some hindering factor? It's the same for God. He can impute His character in the process of justification regardless of your past life as long as you simply say, "Lord I am sorry; please forgive me." He responds, "That's all right," and credits to you His character. But from that moment, He begins literally imparting to us His own character, which isn't an easy thing, and takes a lifetime to complete. Any time I object because the purging/imparting process is too painful, and therefore desire to take the driver's seat, He lets me take over, and I soon find myself in the ditch. "Oops, I goofed again Lord, please take over," and He takes over and drives away. But it isn't long before I say, "I think I will take over again—it seems like easy sailing—and I do and soon we find ourselves in the ditch, again! This is the ongoing process which God pursues in His anxious desire to impart to us His character. This process is only possible as we remove the hindrances. God doesn't send trials and temptations, but He *permits* them. Nevertheless, our challenge isn't with the trial or temptation, but with what the Word says about that problem and the means by which God addresses it—that's where we really stumble, that which is the pruning process. God uses any problem—any trial, any temptation, any hardship—the devil confronts us with, to point us to the solution, which is always *Jesus* in one way or the other. But we prefer other answers. In my studies with people I've heard them say, "Don't you have any other answers?" "No, the answer is Jesus." "Don't you know of any other solution?" "No, the solution is Jesus." It is so much easier to accept human solutions to our problems. If I can do something to solve the problem on my own, I will certainly take that route first—which is why the religions of the world are so much more attractive to the human mind.

Notes:

[13] Ellen G. White, cited in *Messages to Young People, p. 118.*
[14] W. W. Prescott, *Victory In Christ* (Washington, D.C.: Review & Herald Publishing Association,), p. 17.
[15] Ibid.

Study Questions:

1. How do you think the disciples felt when they heard that their nation wasn't the "True Vine"? In what ways might people be making the same mistake in our day? Is it possible that you are placing more confidence in the church you attend than Jesus?

2. In what way does the Bible do the pruning? (34)

3. What does it mean for us to abide in Jesus and for Jesus to abide in us? (35)

4. What does it mean to put God in the driver's seat? How easy is it to take back control? (36,37)

5. What is the essential task of the branch? (38)

6. How is it possible to abide and yet not abide in Jesus? (39)

7. What is the fruit? (41)

8. What gets in the way of purging? (41,42)

9. Why is detaching necessary? (42)

10. Why does Jesus find it hard to give us His victory? (44)

11. What hindering factors may exist in your life that are preventing God from accomplishing His purposes in your life? (45)

Chapter 4

ABIDING "AS I"

"I am the True Vine and My Father is the Husbandman. Every branch in Me that beareth not fruit He taketh away; and every branch that beareth fruit He purgeth it, that it may bring forth more fruit. Now ye are clean through the word which I have spoken unto you. Abide in Me, and I in you. As the branch cannot bear fruit of itself, except it abide in the vine; no more can ye, except ye abide in Me. I am the Vine, ye are the branches: He that abideth in Me, and I in him, the same bringeth forth much fruit: for without Me ye can do nothing. If a man abide not in Me, he is cast forth as a branch, and is withered; and men gather them, and cast them into the fire, and they are burned. If ye abide in Me, and My words abide in you, ye shall ask what ye will, and it shall be done unto you. Herein is My Father glorified, that ye bear much fruit; so shall ye be My disciples" (John 15:1-8).

I hope it doesn't seem repetitious that we keep reading through these verses, for they are vitally important and should be of keen interest to us. Remember as well that this parable comes at the beginning of the final conversation that Jesus had with His disciples, which we find in John 15, 16, and 17. He spoke these words after He left the upper room and headed out into the night. This conversation, His last conversation with the disciples prior to His arrest in the Garden of Gethsemane, couldn't have taken more than two hours, during which He shared some of His most important lessons. Have you ever found yourself similarly needing to give a vast amount of instruction to a loved one? Jesus needed to, and in a very short amount of time, and He tried to pack in as much as possible.

He started with the experience of the vine and the branches. He said, "I am the True Vine, and My Father is the Husbandman" (John 15:1). This was the first time Jesus had ever spoken of this with His disciples, and it came as new information to them, since they were Jews and like all Jews had always looked at the vine as a symbol of themselves. Now Jesus was in effect saying, "That's not correct! 'I am the True Vine, and my Father is the Husbandman. Every branch in Me that beareth not fruit He taketh away: and every branch that beareth fruit He purgeth it, that it may bring forth more fruit'" (John 15:2).

Jesus probably spoke these words at this time for a number of reasons. For one thing, He knew the disciples were going to soon experience important purging, and they didn't even know what needed purging!

Now recall that the agent of purging for the disciples was going to be the Word, and at this point in their spiritual journey, the disciples had not understood the Word—the teachings of their Master, Jesus—nor had the Word accomplished its work yet. There is still the same problem in our day. We have the Scriptures—the Word—but it doesn't do us any good unless we are willing to believe it and allow it to work in us.

The disciples had listened to the Word many times and responded, "That's interesting! That's wonderful!" But they didn't understand the wonderful words they were hearing. We often find ourselves in the same boat. Thousands of people read the Word, believe they will get something from what they are reading, gain a little, but don't understand it at all. The disciples were like this, and Jesus therefore instructed them. As a result, they were going to be able to soon experience the gift of the Holy Spirit, which was to accomplish one thing: dwell on the Word in order to enlighten the disciples, helping them to understand and apply it.

Now He said, "Ye are clean through the word" (John 15:3), and meant they were clean by believing in the lessons that He had spoken to them. The only way to be cleansed is through the Word, which is a spiritual cleansing; that's the only way a human being can be cleansed! Cleansing does not come by way of baptism, for baptism is only an outward symbol.

Then Jesus continued, saying, "Abide in Me, and I in you. As the branch cannot bear fruit of itself, except it abide in the vine; no more can ye, except ye abide in Me. I am the Vine, ye are the branches: He that abideth in Me, and I in him, the same bringeth forth much fruit: for without Me ye can do nothing" (John 15:4, 5).

Flawed Mutual Support

We find a profound lesson in these short verses: no branch can support another branch! Isn't that interesting? Every branch is supposed to bear its own fruit, and the production of fruit points back to the Source of that fruit and creates a desire in another branch to bear fruit as well. And when the fruit is recognized, and the Source of the fruit is also known, then another branch is grafted in and receives its ability to bear fruit from the same original Source as the other branches, which of course is not from another branch. Branches cannot support each other.

Jesus went on in verse six, "If a man abide not in Me, he is cast forth as a branch, and is withered; and men gather them, and cast them into the fire, and they are burned." We've talked about this verse before, so we won't spend any time discussing it now.

Can We Really Ask for Anything?

In verse seven we find the words that we are going to focus on: "If ye abide in Me, and My words abide in you, ye shall ask what you will, and it shall be done unto you" (John 15:7). These words, "Ye shall ask what you will, and it shall be done unto you," are often quoted and taken completely out of context as a promise that can be claimed to cover a vast number of things.

If we carefully examine this verse, we will find that certain limiting conditions are connected with it. What might these limiting conditions be? The production of fruit? Whether one abides or not? Whether we abide in Him, or He abides in us? These are good responses, but it is important to find the *right* response, since we give so little thought to this promise that is so easily claimed.

It helps to consider the context of this verse—a parable about a Vine, and a branch whose sole purpose is to produce fruit. It also helps to remember that the branch merely functions as a channel through which the Vine produces fruit. Would it be fair to suggest then, that if the branch were to ask for something of the Vine, it would only be asking for one thing: to bear more fruit, which is the only thing a branch could do, and which, accordingly, is all it would be asking? It wouldn't be asking to build a house, or to take a trip, or to do anything else. Would it? The branch would not be concerned about any of these things. It would be saying, "Lord, produce more fruit in me"—that would be its only request.

Do you see how logical this is? Would you agree that it would be foolish to apply this promise to anything and everything that might come into our minds? How foolish we are. We have stretched God's Word and attempted to make it encompass everything. Many a preacher has quoted this verse and suggested that God will do whatever you ask, as long as you are sincere and ask in the right way. But God isn't in that kind of business, and neither is the branch. The branch is only going to ask for more fruit, and the Husbandman is going to respond by starting the only process that enables the branch to bear more fruit: purging.

What Kind of Fruit Are We Asking For?

Now the only kind of fruit we are asking for is that which will develop God's character in us! We were created for one purpose: to reflect the image of Jesus. We may think a Cadillac parked in the garage will help us reflect His image, but God has a different idea. Would you agree, then, that these verses are not about asking God for things? They are about asking God to use us as branches for what He intended in the first place: to perfectly reflect His image. The Cadillac doesn't keep me from being a branch, but neither does the Cadillac make me a branch or cause me to bear fruit. Character is the fruit that God will grant, as we ask for it and as our minds are open to receive it.

It goes without saying that God does not force His character upon anyone, even though we were expressly created to bear the perfect image of Jesus. Bearing the image is very possible, but doing so necessitates a willingness to be purged. In order to bear fruit, God sends us back to the Word that it might have its perfect work in us. That means we do more than just read the Word and then forget about what we have perused. No, we endure the purging as it cuts! The Bible describes the Word as being sharper than any two-edged sword and speaks of it dividing asunder. And that's what it does—it separates and divides—it separates us from the world and the things of the world, and changes our interest in the world. That Word also puts the desire in our hearts to make God first. Jesus said, "Seek ye first the Kingdom of God, and His righteousness," (Matthew 6:33) something that is only possible as God dwells in us.

Fruit-bearing, Glorifying God, and Discipleship

"If ye abide in Me, and My words abide in you, ye shall ask what you will, and it shall be done unto you. Herein is My Father glorified. . . ." (John 15:7, 8, first part).

This is interesting because verse eight heads right into the fruit-bearing business. "Herein is My Father glorified, that ye bear much fruit"! Notice that our asking and the Father being glorified through fruit-bearing are connected: "Ye shall ask what you will. . . . Herein is My Father glorified, that ye bear much fruit." So, asking whatever you want, then, is asking for God to be glorified, and He is only glorified when we bear fruit.

Reading again, this time notice the last part of the verse: "Ask what you will, and it shall be done unto you. Herein is My Father glorified, that ye bear much fruit; *so shall ye be My disciples*." Did you notice it said, "So shall ye be My disciples"? Whoever thought discipleship and fruit-bearing were connected?

Branches Attaching to Other Branches

It's worth noting in passing that a disciple is one who is taught. You may recall that Paul sent his first epistle to the Corinthian church when he heard disturbing news about ongoing contentions: "For it hath been declared unto me of you, my brethren, by them which are of the house of Chloe, that there are contentions among you. Now this I say, that every one of you saith, I am of Paul; and I of Apollos; and I of Cephas; and I of Christ. Is Christ divided? Was Paul crucified for you? Or were ye baptized in the name of Paul?" (1 Corinthians 1:11-13).

Did you notice what was going on? Did you notice that the people in Corinth were succumbing to one of the greatest weaknesses of human beings? What was that weakness? Branches were attaching themselves to other branches, instead of attaching themselves to the Vine. We have already learned that a branch cannot support another branch—it is not possible—but the people in Corinth were trying to. So one person was saying, "I'm a disciple of Paul"; another was saying, "I'm a disciple of Apollos"; and so forth.

In our day we hear different names, but the same thing is going on. One person says, "I'm a disciple of Luther"; another person says, "I'm a disciple of Wesley." Down through history, people have been attaching themselves to this one and that one, and it's still going on in our day. Think about the last time you were in church listening to the sermon. Did it take you much time to figure out where the pastor was trained? And, if we weren't embarrassed to say so, we might even find ourselves saying, "I'm a disciple of so and so." The apostle Paul recognized this tendency, for we find him saying, Don't even say you are of Paul, because I didn't die for you.

The branch only has one purpose. What is that purpose? To bear fruit that reflects the Vine! Attached to the Vine, branches will attract other branches to the Vine instead of to themselves. Unless our work, unless all of our work, attracts men and women to Jesus Christ, it is worthless—in fact worse than worthless.

What Constitutes a Disciple?

Sadly, the one factor that has done more to slow down Christianity than any other is that men have taken pride in their ability to attract followers. And the result has been branches attaching themselves to other branches. There have been great Christian leaders down through history who were marvelous men, and many of them built great empires. When these people passed off the scene of action, their empire still existed, and the question arose as to what was to be done with it. Drop it? No! The followers carried on the teachings and interpretations of the founder, and the result was failure. Why? Because personal interpretation prevents the Word from doing its work. There is a danger here for all pastors. Pastors must attract their hearers back to the Word and to the Lord Jesus Christ, for it is in the Word and the Lord Jesus Christ that new life is experienced.

As we continue, Jesus said, "So shall ye be My disciples" (John 15:8). What constitutes a disciple of Christ? One whose life conforms to Jesus' teaching. What can be the only sign of discipleship, then? A life that reflects the character of Jesus. And what are we doing when we reflect the character of Jesus? We are telling the world that we believe in Jesus and have completely accepted Him as Lord and Master.

Understanding Jesus' Words

Now in John 15:9 we find Jesus' words: "As the Father hath loved Me, so have I loved you."

Have you ever thought about what Jesus was saying here? Here are some of the pertinent facts: He was speaking at the very end of His life; He was going to die in just a few short hours; and the disciples were going to completely misunderstand what was going on. In spite of all that, we find Him saying, "As the Father hath loved Me, so have I loved you: continue ye in My love" (John 15:9).

Have you ever tried to share something with someone who doesn't believe what you are talking about, and find as a consequence that the individual not only misunderstands, but doesn't get the message at all? If you have, then you can appreciate the challenge Jesus was facing. He said, "As the Father has loved Me, so I have loved you: continue ye in My love."

In just a few hours the disciples were going to see their beloved Master hanging on the cross. What would keep them from thinking the Father didn't love them? What would prevent them from misapplying what they thought they had heard Jesus saying—but didn't understand—and therefore from completely misunderstanding His death? What would keep this misunderstanding from occurring? His words! Their hope would be in His words. What were those words? The words that He had been telling them all along regarding the things that would happen. That's why He said, "These things have I told you, that when the time shall come, ye may remember that I told you of them" (John 16:4).

Are We Abiding?

Here Jesus was bringing up a subject that not only greatly confused them, but one they resisted even hearing about. Jesus went right on: ". . . continue ye in My love. If ye keep My commandments, ye shall abide in My love; even as I have kept My Father's commandments, and abide in His love" (John 15:9, 10). The Lord Jesus Christ had come to planet Earth because His Father had sent Him, and He had willingly volunteered to take on the role of Saviour of mankind. Therefore the Scriptures can rightly say, ". . . God was in Christ, reconciling the world unto Himself" (2 Corinthians 5:19). So Jesus said, "As the Father hath loved me, so have I loved you: continue ye in My love. If ye keep My commandments, ye shall abide in My love; even as I have kept My Father's commandments, and abide in His love" (John 15:9, 10). Then Jesus proceeded to list the commandments in the next few verses:

> *"These things have I spoken unto you, that My joy might remain in you, and that your joy might be full. This is My commandment, That ye love one another, as I have loved you"* *(John 15:11,12).*

This commandment indicates whether I am abiding in Christ or not.

"As I!"

Now go back to John 15:10, where Jesus says, "If ye keep My commandments, ye shall abide in My love; even as I have kept My Father's commandments, and abide in His love." Here we find the key words that explain the meaning of the Vine and the branch. What are they? "As I"! "Do this as I!" These two words will answer every question a person might have regarding the Christian experience. "How can I bear this?" "As I." Jesus answers every one of our questions with "As I"! Hebrews 4:15 says He "was in *all* points tempted like as we are, yet without sin," and therefore can answer *all* our questions with "As I."

Do you see that abiding in the Vine is all about abiding in the same way that Jesus abided in the Vine? Jesus abided in—trusted—His Father, no matter what was going on. He trusted regardless of whether it was a Gethsemane or a Calvary. As He faced the unknown of the tomb, and in fact couldn't see beyond it, He kept right on trusting. Humanly speaking, this level of trusting was impossible—Gethsemane was so bad that it brought blood to Jesus' brow, and He collapsed and would have died had an angel not been sent to strengthen Him.

Why was Jesus able to endure? Because He was *abiding* in the Vine. And what was this revealing? Character, His unshakable character! Could circumstances change His character? Yes, it could have, but it didn't. Could a change in environment change His character? Yes, it could have, but again, it didn't! Nothing could change His character. And so Jesus said, Abide . . . "even as I." Love "even as I." This was the great lesson!

Jesus didn't simply say, "Here is a good story," or "Here is an illustration." No, He very specifically said, "I am the Vine, ye are the branches. As I have been abiding in my Father and completely depended on Him, so you must do the same thing. "As I." When Jesus came to this world and lived as a branch, He was continually abiding in His Father. In our day, Jesus is the Vine and we are the branches; and we are to receive from Him as He received from His Father. How did He do it? He looked to His Father.

Just think of the difference going to *our* Vine would make with our frustrations? It would completely eliminate them! What do we normally do? We go to some friend and say, "What in the world am I going to do?" Jesus says, "Do what I did!"—that is His answer, and His answer is always so simple. You find the same thing when Jesus said, "Ye are clean through the word that I have spoken unto you."

The Vine's Loving Friendship

> *"Greater love hath no man than this, That a man lay down his life for his friends. Ye are My friends, if ye do whatsoever I command you" (John 15:13,14).*

Jesus was beginning to gently talk with His disciples about giving one's life, because He would be giving His Own life in just a few hours. Now remember, the disciples were convinced that Jesus wasn't going to die—at least their minds were not open to such a possibility at the time. They did not believe He was going to give His life, and were totally shocked when He did. But in this part of His conversation Jesus went beyond talking about the physical part of giving oneself, to also talking about the great love demonstrated in this giving. It is worth noting that this was the first time Jesus spoke to His disciples as "friends."

Notice what Andrew Murray says about this demonstration of love in his book *The True Vine*:

> *"Greater love hath no man than this, that a man lay down his life for his friends. Christ does indeed long to have us know that the secret root and strength of all He is and does for us as the Vine is love. As we learn to believe this, we shall feel that here is something which we not only need to think and know about, but a living power, a divine life which we need to receive within us."*[16]

This love, this form of love—this form of divine love—is a mysterious power and influence that saturates the Scriptures, and is present from Genesis to Revelation. Yet it is of such a subtle nature that it is easy to be confused about it. It doesn't help that modern society has confused our thinking on the subject of love by constantly bombarding us with a counterfeit form of love.

Why are we confused? Because we think the power of love has something to do with emotion—strong emotion—that reveals itself, and is persuasive in its power. True love, however, doesn't demonstrate its power in self-centered persuasiveness, but rather in giving itself; it doesn't manifest itself in receiving, but in giving. Real love is just the opposite of what we see in the world around us, and the epitome of real love according to John 15:13 is laying down one's life for others! Total giving is total loving! Love is never about satisfying self, nor is it about receiving for oneself. It's never about accumulating or hoarding, either; for it is always giving of itself; which is just the opposite of what man thinks.

Quoting Andrew Murray again: "As we learn to believe this, we shall feel that here is something which we not only need to think and know about, but a living power, a divine life which we need to receive within us."[17]

The Branch's Giving Capacity of Love

The giving capacity that characterizes this kind of love is only possible when God dwells within. It goes without saying that self clamors for first place from the very first moment. From that first breath to the final one, self will not only continue to manifest itself, but will grow larger and consider itself more important every step of the way, unless the Lord Jesus is invited to dwell within. This self-centeredness cannot be changed without a new source of life. That is why the old nature has to completely die and the new divine nature invited in, to create something that we human beings are utterly incapable of producing within ourselves.

Christ and His love are inseparable and identical.[18] If you have the one; you have the other; if you lack the one; you lack the other. "Christ and His love are inseparable; they are identical. God is love, and Christ is love. God and Christ and the divine love can only be known by having them. . . ."[19] You won't understand love by knowing about it; you can believe all you want about the love of God but still not understand it; you can write all the poetry you want about love, and you can express your feelings about love and all the other emotions of life, but you still won't understand the love of God. "God and Christ and the divine love can only be known by having them, by Their life and power working within us"[20]—there is no other way! Jesus put it this way: "This is life eternal, that they might know Thee the only true God, and Jesus Christ, Whom Thou hast sent" (John 17:3).

The Highest Measure of Love

Let's consider more of Andrew Murray's words: "Sacrifice is the highest measure of love: When a man gives his life, he holds nothing back, he gives all he has and is. It is this our Lord Jesus wants to make clear to us concerning the mystery of His Vine. . . ."[21]

This constant giving is why Jesus pictures Himself as the Vine. Why? Because the Vine is constantly giving the sap, which is its lifeblood. And it keeps the sap constantly flowing, which of course means it is constantly giving. This illustrates how God gives because it is His nature to give; He can't be God and not give. In the same way, if the branch lives, it also bears fruit. Why? Because it is the branch's nature to bear fruit. The branch *always* bears fruit. It's not a matter of the branch bearing fruit, or not bearing fruit; the branch always bears fruit. How does it bear fruit? By receiving what the Vine provides.

We Bear Fruit No Matter What

Notice, however, if it is true that the branch bears fruit no matter what, but at some point is not receiving sap from the vine, then the resulting fruit will originate from a different source, and will become the *real* problem—the main problem—of the branch! The branch is going to bear fruit, but what kind of fruit is it going to bear? It can choose to receive sap from the True Vine and have the true fruit of the character of Jesus reproduced in its life, or it can choose to receive sap from a false, pseudo-substitute source and bear a false, substitute fruit.

Friendship With the Vine

Now Jesus said that we are His friends if we do whatever He commands us. This word "friend" is totally misunderstood. We say we have a host of friends, but that's not really true. Someone said we have many acquaintances in a lifetime, but few friends. I believe that, and would therefore suggest that saying "We have a host of acquaintances" would be more accurate.

It has been suggested that the definition of a true friend is someone who knows all about us and loves us just the same. Can this definition be applied to the people around us? Hardly! The only person to whom this definition applies is Jesus. In John 15:15 Jesus said, "Henceforth, I call you not servants; for the servant knoweth not what his Lord doeth: but I have called you friends; for all things that I have heard of My Father I have made known unto you." Jesus called us friends. A true friend knows all about you. With this kind of friend there are no secrets; nothing is hidden. That's why we don't have many "true" friends. We have friends, but these are often surface friendships because we don't share the deeper things on our hearts with them. For many of us, the only time we can honestly open our hearts is when we are on our knees, praying.

But notice again Jesus' words in John 15:15, "Henceforth I call you not servants; for the servant knoweth not what his Lord doeth." Here Jesus was talking to His disciples as friends. Why? Because they were soon going to face a situation that would be unlike anything they had faced before; a situation they could not endure without advance warning; a situation requiring Jesus to open His heart and clearly reveal what was going to take place.

Serving Two Masters?

We must acknowledge that the Bible frequently uses the term "servants" in describing our relationship to the Lord, and this deserves some consideration. Matthew 6:24 says, "No man can serve two masters." Modifying that slightly, "No man can be a servant to two masters." Consider as well that in Bible times, a servant was almost always a slave. And so we get the following, "No man can be a slave to two masters."

Now God wants us to be slaves from the standpoint of our not needing to understand everything in order to believe. Why? Because what a person does must be of faith, for as Romans 14:23 puts it, "Whatsoever is not of faith is sin." This means that God enables us to constantly exercise our faith, since He doesn't tell us about everything ahead of time. Yet He never allows our faith to be tested beyond that which we can bear.

Now the disciples were coming to a point in their experience when their faith was going to be greatly tested. I don't think we can remotely appreciate what they were facing: They had been with Jesus for three and a half years; He was soon going to be hanging from a tree in front of them; and their faith was going to fail them. We know this because when it happened, they fled and completely left Him. In fact, all the disciples were soon hiding behind locked doors in the upper room, and would have remained hidden, and remained unbelievers, had not Jesus pursued them following His resurrection, revealed Himself, reminded them of what was going on, and helped them put all the pieces together.

But fear and unbelief wasn't what Jesus preferred for His disciples. He would have been pleased had they understood and believed from the beginning. Had He not already spoken of His pending death? Had He not already told the Jewish people through the prophet Isaiah the manner in which He was going to die? But the disciples had their own ideas about what was going to happen, and therefore misunderstood statements that should have been completely clear.

Knowing All Things

When Jesus was speaking of true friendship, He was referring to the highest possible form of spiritual experience, which comes through the indwelling of the Holy Spirit.

Jesus said, "Henceforth, I call you not servants; for the servant knoweth not what his lord doeth: but I have called you friends; for all things that I have heard of My Father I have made known unto you" (John 15:15).

Have you ever thought about what Jesus was communicating when He said, "All things that I have heard of My Father I have made known unto you"? He was God's perfect mouthpiece on Earth, and was saying, "All things that I have heard of My Father I have made known unto you." I marvel when I think about this, because as Jesus was faithful to His Father, so He wants us to be faithful to Him; and faithfulness is how discipleship is revealed. Remember the words in John 15:8, "Herein is My Father glorified, that ye bear much fruit; so shall ye be My disciples." Christ was in effect saying, My Father told Me these things; now I am sharing them with you.

Responding to the Vine

How are we going to respond to Christ's plea? Ignore it? Listen, but continue on without anything changing? Listen, but only drowsily respond? The answer comes as we consider His commission to us. What commission did He give us? Wasn't it bearing fruit? That was Jesus' commission. Will He do the same thing in us? Yes! He is going to bear the fruit of His Own character in us—that's the purpose of fruit-bearing and His stated objective for us.

Unfortunately, too often when God speaks to us about fruit-bearing, our first thought is to go to our neighbors and say, "Hey, you better get ready because Jesus is coming!" Too often they react with a "Really? Do you believe it? You certainly don't look like you do! I don't see anything different between us." Would you agree that people shouldn't need to be *told* that Jesus is coming; rather they should *know* He is coming by the way we live?

An Attainable Life

Is this kind of living attainable, or is more being expected of us than is possible? It shouldn't be, and it won't be, if our fruit-bearing comes as a result of Christ dwelling within us. Why? Because as a result of the indwelling presence of Jesus, God's character will be seen in us, just as God's character was seen in Christ. Do you remember how Jesus responded to Philip's request, "Show us the Father"? He answered, "Have I been so long time with you, and yet hast thou not known Me, Philip? He that hath seen Me hath seen the Father; and how sayest thou then, Show us the Father?" (John 14:8, 9).

If Christ is dwelling in us, is it too much to expect that He'll be able to say, "If you have seen Mrs. Smith, or Brother Jones, you have seen Me"?

Notes:

[16] Ibid., p. 143.
[17] Ibid.
[18] Ibid.
[19] Ibid.
[20] Ibid.
[21] Ibid., p. 144.

Study Questions:

1. What is the branch asking for when it asks for something from the Vine? (49)

2. What kind of fruit will the branch develop? (50)

3. What two words answer every question of the Christian experience, and why? (48)

4. When a man gives his life, how much does he give. What do we learn about from the Vine? (56)

5. How do we sometimes mistakenly seek to bear fruit? (60)

6. How is fruit-bearing possible? (60)

Chapter 5

Abiding and Reflecting Christ's Character

"As the Father hath loved me, so have I loved you: continue ye in My love. If ye keep My commandments, ye shall abide in My love; even as I have kept My Father's commandments, and abide in His love. These things have I spoken unto you, that My joy might remain in you, and that your joy might be full. This is My commandment, That ye love one another, as I have loved you. Greater love hath no man than this, That a man lay down his life for his friends" (John 15:9-13).

We have been studying John 15 for quite some time, and continue because it is the heart of the concentrated bits of counsel that Jesus gave His disciples just before He entered Gethsemane and gave His life as a ransom for many. We've been talking about the Vine and the branch, and the need to abide.

This time we are going to examine John 15:9-13. Let's start with verses 7 and 8:

"If ye abide in Me, and My words abide in you, ye shall ask what ye will, and it shall be done unto you. Herein is My Father glorified, that ye bear much fruit; so shall ye be My disciples" (John 15:7, 8).

It's important for us to remember that a disciple is someone who is not only taught by Jesus, but who also reflects His teaching in daily life. As we bear fruit, God classifies us as His disciples.

As the Father Loved Me

Continuing in John 15:9, Jesus said:

"As the Father hath loved me, so have I loved you: continue ye in My love."

These verses have a tendency to slip away into sentimental nothingness for the simple reason that our concept of Biblical love is theoretical and not practical, to say nothing of the fact that what the world feels about physical love influences our understanding of love. Needless to say, there is a significant difference between what the world says about love and what the Bible says about love, and we find it hard to separate the two. But Jesus helped us when He added the words, "As the Father hath loved Me." What was Jesus saying? What meaning should we attach to His words? It's very difficult to express the depth of what He was saying by using human terminology, let alone to fully understand it.

Demonstrating God's Character

But there is a thought here that we haven't touched on yet and which deserves our attention. Return with me in your minds to the time when sin manifested itself in Heaven. How did evil originate and develop? It originated in the heart of Satan and manifested itself against God, particularly in attacking His character. Why? Because God's character was love, and was explained as love to the created beings in Heaven. In our day it isn't hard for us to recognize the difference between the loving nature of God's character and Satan's nature of evil. But where sin did not exist, where there was only perfect holiness and innocence, explaining God's character of love was very difficult. God could say, "My character is love," but so could the angelic beings, for there was no way to compare God's love with Satan's evil.

Well, the Devil took advantage of the situation to strongly challenge God's character, and the ensuing controversy made a tremendous impact on the angels, and resulted in much discussion and great consternation in Heaven relative to what was going on. The angels were in doubt as to who was right. What was this love and how could it be proven? Was God right? Was Satan right? Eventually war broke out in Heaven over this controversy, and Satan and those who sided with him were cast out, as we find described in Revelation 12.

Preplanning

This controversy and the resulting sin did not come as a surprise to God, for in His foreknowledge He had known what was going to happen ahead of time and made preparations to meet the challenge. We have a limited understanding of what dealing with Lucifer and sin meant to God, but even from our limited perspective we recognize that God was manifesting His character of love from the beginning, and will continue to manifest His love to the end. Only a character of love like God's could have created a being like Lucifer, and poured over him all the glory possible, without thinking about a future time when a large segment of the angels would be turned against God.

Would you have created a being with Satan's potential if you would have been God? We can't comprehend what God was doing, but God lovingly created not only the heavenly inhabitants, but also the inhabitants of this earth and untold other worlds. When Satan raised the challenge, God activated the plan that allowed one Person to represent and fully reveal His character. Imagine if you were on trial for something that could bring life or death consequences, and were forced to select one person to perfectly represent your character, how careful would you be? In God's case it was even a little more complicated, because this Person needed to perfectly represent all three members of the Godhead—we will use the term "Triune God"—to the universe.

A Representative Role

We know that Jesus was selected for this representative role before sin broke out. It would be His difficult task to represent God's character to created beings—angels and all the other inhabitants of the universe—who needed to know about God and His character of love. This representation was also necessary, since the foundation of God's universe was love and needed to be knit together on that foundation. Needless to say, the love that everything would be founded upon would have to be more than a sentimental attitude, for it was the principle upon which rested all the power of God. The Triune God chose Jesus Christ to make that representation.

Our Role

How do we integrate Jesus' task of representing the Father's character of love with His words to the disciples in John 15:9, "As the Father hath loved Me, so have I loved you"? Jesus is admonishing us to represent His character to the fallen inhabitants of our planet and the inhabitants of the rest of the universe. We have been called to make the same representation that Jesus was called to make. As we properly represent Jesus on a practical basis, His character will be revealed, known, and understood. And what intellectually impacts the inhabitants of unfallen worlds will bring practical transformation to the fallen inhabitants of our world. This demonstration will enable fallen people to become new creatures; it will allow them to experience complete transformation—this was God's objective for the plan of atonement from the beginning, and this is what Jesus had in mind when He said, "As the Father hath loved Me, so have I loved you: continue ye in My love."

When Jesus said, "Continue ye in My love," He was obviously referring to His Own love, but He was also referring to a chain reaction of love: God loved Jesus Christ, Jesus Christ loved human beings, and human beings were to love one another. This is how love operates, and God's love will be seen when we love each other.

Continuing in Love
A Practical Demonstration

There's a quotation found in *Christ's Object Lessons,* page 120, that we should consider in passing. In contemplating these thoughts we must remember that the only church that was completely true to God was the church of Ephesus. Every other church failed, and even the Ephesus church had problems, but because this church did God's work God's way, it became a miracle-working church. The amount of work accomplished by the members of that church in spite of daunting circumstances was phenomenal!

In the chapter on the Pearl of Great Price, we read the following:

> *"Then the glad tidings of a risen Saviour were carried to the uttermost bounds of the inhabited world. The church beheld converts flocking to her from all directions. Believers were reconverted. Sinners united with Christians in seeking the Pearl of great price. The prophecy was fulfilled, The weak shall be 'as David,' and the house of David 'as the angel of the Lord." Zechariah 12:8. Every Christian saw in his brother the divine similitude of benevolence and love. One interest prevailed. One object swallowed up all others. All hearts beat in harmony. The only ambition of the believers was to reveal the likeness of Christ's character, and to labor for the*

enlargement of His kingdom. 'The multitude of them that believed were of one heart and of one soul. . . . With great power gave the apostles witness of the resurrection of the Lord Jesus; and great grace was upon them all.' Acts 4:32,33. 'And the Lord added to the church daily such as should be saved.' Acts 2:47. The Spirit of Christ animated the whole congregation; for they had found the Pearl of great price."

"These scenes are to be repeated, and with greater power. The outpouring of the Holy Spirit on the Day of Pentecost was the former rain, but the latter rain will be more abundant."[21]

Let's look at this quotation carefully. First notice what quickly happened: "Then the glad tidings of a risen Saviour were carried to the uttermost bounds of the inhabited world." Paul also testified of this in his Epistle to the Colossians when he said the Gospel was carried to the uttermost parts of the earth in his lifetime (see Colossians 1:23). I remember my mother and others before her day speaking of finishing the work in their lifetime. In our day, there is still the desire to carry the Gospel to the rest of the world in our lifetime. Will we succeed? I don't think there is much hope unless we start doing things God's way. When that happens, the work will be quickly completed.

Reading again, "Then the glad tidings of a risen Saviour were carried to the uttermost bounds of the inhabited world. The church beheld converts flocking to her from all directions." That's a switch! Wouldn't it be something if we only had to open the doors of our churches and people would flock in? It's quite different in our day. Now we visit people, plead with them to study, invite them to meetings, and advertise—we do anything and everything we can to attract people to our churches. But that wasn't God's way in the church of Ephesus. It says the church beheld converts flocking to her from all directions. Not only that, it says, "believers were reconverted." Here lost, backslidden, believers were returning and being reconverted. The church was doing God's work God's way, and as a result God was blessing.

"Believers were reconverted. Sinners united with Christians in seeking the Pearl of great price. The prophecy was fulfilled, The weak shall be 'as David,' and the house of David 'as the angel of the Lord.' Zechariah 12:8. Every Christian saw in his brother the divine similitude of benevolence and love."[22]

"As the Father hath loved me, so have I loved you: continue ye in My love" (John 15:9). Have you ever seen a church with that kind of love? Churches need that kind of love on a general basis, and the members —each one of us—need it on a personal basis, too. What a difference it would make if our churches were like the Ephesus church. If every one of our members—if every Christian—saw in his brothers and sisters the divine similitude of benevolent love, every trace of criticism would be banished.

Benevolent Love

You may be asking, "What is this benevolent love?" Benevolent love is a holy love, it is a giving love, it is a divine love. Earthly love is usually just the opposite, isn't it? It is selfish; it loves in order to receive love, and there is usually a selfish motive behind it. By way of contrast, benevolent love gives without expecting anything in return. Have you ever experienced that kind of love? Every believer experienced that kind of love in Ephesus. Today, when somebody does something nice, invariably someone is going to be saying, "Ha, I wonder what he's after?" Or, "I know why she did that!"

These suspicions were nonexistent in the church of Ephesus, for "every Christian saw in his brother the divine similitude of benevolence and love. One interest prevailed. One object swallowed up all others. . . ." What was that object? It was the one we have been studying about, the one object that prevailed then, the one object that will prevail again. What was it? It was to reveal the righteousness of Christ's character. "One interest prevailed. One object swallowed up all others. All hearts beat in harmony." Isn't that beautiful? "All hearts beat in harmony. The only ambition of the believers was to reveal the likeness of Christ's character. . . ." Did you notice that? The ambition of the believers wasn't to outdo one another; their only ambition was to reveal the character of Christ—there was no competition! Every believer was only seeking to do one thing: to reveal the likeness of Jesus perfectly! And then it goes on to say, "and to labor for the enlargement of [Christ's] kingdom. 'The multitude of them that believed were of one heart and of one soul . . . . With great power gave the apostles witness of the resurrection of the Lord Jesus; and great grace was upon them all.' (Acts 4:32, 33)."

Reflecting Christ's Character

Did you notice what was upon them? Grace. What was this grace? Christ's character. Let me back that up with the following quotation from Christ's Object Lessons: "To learn of Christ means to receive His grace, which is His character."[23] There are many references along this line, but this is probably the clearest one. So what was being described when we read that "great grace was upon them all"? We are reading about a church where the character of Christ was strongly implanted upon the members.

This implanting explains why the people looking upon the Ephesus church members knew that they had been with Jesus. These believers were true disciples and were reflecting their Teacher; they were doing what disciples are supposed to do. Whose character were they reflecting? Christ's! As a result, their characters were molded in such a way that they continually reminded others of Jesus. I can hear bystanders saying "Why, that's what Jesus was like." Are people saying that about us in our day? Should that be happening in our day? Absolutely, and when it happens, people will flock to the church—you won't be able to hold them back, and it will surely happen! We read further, "'And the Lord added to the church daily such as should be saved' (Acts 2:47). The Spirit of Christ animated the whole congregation; for they had found the Pearl of great price."[24]

With Great Power

Notice the next sentence: "These scenes are to be repeated, and with greater power." Isn't that thrilling? "The outpouring of the Holy Spirit on the Day of Pentecost was the former rain [and was wonderful], but the latter rain will be even more abundant."[25] If nothing else thrills us, this should; and we can't help but ask, "What is holding things up?" Ephesians 1:3, 4 is an important text in this regard:

> "Blessed be the God and Father of our Lord Jesus Christ, Who hath blessed us with all spiritual blessings in heavenly places in Christ: According as He hath chosen us in Him before the foundation of the world, that we should be holy and without blame before Him in love" (Ephesians 1:3, 4).

God selected Christ to be His representative before the foundations of the world were laid. It wasn't easy for God to put the plan into motion. God struggled with the decision. But Jesus volunteered to represent God to humankind, and now we have been chosen in Jesus to do the same thing. Ephesians 1:4 says, ". . . He hath chosen us in Him before the foundation of the world, that we should be holy and without blame before Him in love."

As Jesus stood before the Father in love and reflected His character, so we are to stand before Jesus in perfect love and reflect His character, in order that the world might be attracted to Him through us. This is the way God planned it in the heavenly council, and it's the only way the controversy over His character is ever going to be resolved. Just as Jesus was a living demonstration of God's love, so Jesus has chosen us to be living demonstrations of His love—living proof of the validity of what He accomplished on the cross. Just as God had no other means of revealing Himself to humankind than Jesus, so Jesus has no other means of revealing Himself to humankind than through you and me!

Becoming a "Fool" for Christ

The disciples didn't understand, didn't remotely understand, what was going to take place soon, and the people observing Jesus dying on the cross were not going to understand either. So Jesus was warning the disciples about His forthcoming death to keep their confidence in Him from being completely shaken. Jesus also knew the people looking on would consider Him a fool! Did it matter to Him what people would be thinking? No! Should it matter to us what people think of us? No! Paul said he would gladly be labeled a fool for following Christ, and anyone giving his heart to the Lord Jesus Christ in our day is also going to be considered a fool in the eyes of the world—you may think otherwise, but you are mistaken for the world hasn't become more accepting of those who surrender their lives to Jesus in our day than they did in His!

Jesus was viewed as a total fool in the eyes of the people of His day, sadly even by those who considered themselves His followers. When He was hanging on the cross, it was His followers who were saying, "We thought He was the One Who was going to deliver us." But while they were hanging their heads in disbelief, He was saving them! Do you think people are going to understand if you completely consecrate yourself to God and let Him remake you into a new creature? They won't! They will think you are a fool; they will say you're being fanatical; they will say you are making too great a sacrifice. Only when self has been totally crucified is it possible to make such a surrender, and patiently endure the world's disdain.

Predestined for God's Family

Paul continues, saying:

> *"Having predestinated us unto the adoption of children by Jesus Christ to Himself, according to the good pleasure of His will, to the praise of the glory of His grace, wherein He hath made us accepted in the Beloved"* (Ephesians 1:5, 6).

Let's look at these words in greater detail. "Having predestinated us . . ." Who is this? God the Father. What does the word "predestinated" mean? Preplanned; planned ahead of time. So, God preplanned. Now we need to be clear that preplanning didn't mean that God was insisting that things turn out a certain way. Nor are we suggesting that He would manipulate circumstances to only allow one outcome. However, He preplanned—He made provision—that every person could have a place in His family as adopted children. How? "Adoption of children by Jesus Christ to Himself, according to the good pleasure of His will" (Ephesians 1:5).

God desired to bring the universe into perfect harmony, "to the praise and glory of [notice] His grace." There's that word "grace" again. Do you remember what we learned about it? Do you remember what word can be substituted in its place? "Character." According to what we learned "grace" is God's character. So we can read Ephesians 1:6 as follows: "to the praise and glory of His character." The word "character" makes perfect sense, since God was choosing Jesus Christ to demonstrate and reflect His character to the universe. What was the purpose of His plan then? Learning to love God on the basis of His character of love.

When we say, "To know Him is to love Him," we are not referring to sentimental love. John said, "He that loveth not, knoweth not God" (1 John 4:8). If you know God, you will love Him; if you don't know Him, you won't love Him. You may have heard about Him—heard lots about Him, but if you don't know Him, you won't love Him. To know God is to love Him; you can't help but love Him if you know Him!

"In Whom we have redemption through His blood, the forgiveness of sins, according to the riches of His grace; wherein He hath abounded toward us in all wisdom and prudence. . . ." (Ephesians 1:7, 8).

The first chapter of Ephesians is probably the richest chapter in all Scripture when it comes to unfolding God's plan of salvation. The summary provided for us in Ephesians recaptures what Jesus was telling His disciples only hours before He died on the cross. In His remaining twenty-four hours, Jesus needed to have a very serious conversation with His disciples. What would you say if you only had six hours to communicate your final thoughts to your loved ones? I'm guessing little time would be spent talking about the piano or the automobile.

Keeping God's Commandments

"If ye keep My commandments, ye shall abide in My love; even as I have kept My Father's commandments, and abide in His love" (John 15:10).

We desperately need to get away from the idea that commandment-keeping and reflecting the image of Jesus are the same thing. They may be similar at some level, but our understanding of them is different, and our practical application of them should also be different. One of the reasons we lump commandment-keeping and reflecting Christ's image together is that our concept of keeping the Ten Commandments is so inadequate.

In John 15:10 Jesus was talking about love. Notice the words recorded in John 15:12, where we find Him saying, "Love one another, as I have loved you." He was in effect saying, "I have reflected the character of My Father. I have revealed Him, and I have completed the task that He gave Me. God asked Me to reflect His image in perfectly representing His character to the universe. Now you do the same thing, reflecting My image even as I reflected His image. Do this if you love Me."

Were His thoughts limited to Sabbathkeeping? Was He admonishing against theft or prevarication? Was He rebuking adultery? They were included, but keeping His commandments encompassed so much more than the "dos" and "don'ts" that we so often think of. Not breaking the Sabbath, not stealing or telling lies, not committing adultery, all of these are to be as far away from our lives as they were from Christ's life on Earth—they shouldn't enter into our minds in even the slightest way, and we're not talking about being sanctimonious, either. Rather, we are simply talking about the new life that is experienced when Jesus is allowed to dwell within.

Does victory come through resolve and struggle? Is it the kind of thing where you decide to be truthful, grit your teeth, and resist the temptation? I can almost hear someone quoting *Thoughts From the Mount of Blessing*, page 141, where it says, "The Christian life is a battle and a march," and there are a lot of people who are fighting the Devil every inch of the way, and they look battle scared. But what does it really say?

> "The Christian life is a battle and a march. But the victory to be gained is not won by human power. The field of conflict is the domain of the heart. The battle which we have to fight—the greatest battle that was ever fought by man—is the surrender of self to the will of God, the yielding of the heart to the sovereignty of love. The old nature, born of blood and of the will of the flesh, cannot inherit the Kingdom of God. The hereditary tendencies, the former habits, must be given up.
>
> "He who determines to enter the spiritual kingdom will find that all the powers and passions of an unregenerate nature, backed by the forces of the kingdom of darkness, are arrayed against him. Selfishness and pride will make a stand against anything that would show them to be sinful. We cannot, of ourselves, conquer the evil desires and habits that strive for the mastery. We cannot overcome the mighty foe who holds us in his thrall. God alone can give us the victory. He desires us to have the mastery over ourselves, our own will and ways. But He cannot work in us without our consent and cooperation. The divine Spirit works through the faculties and powers given to man. Our energies are required to cooperate with God.
>
> "The victory is not won without much earnest prayer, without the humbling of self at every step. Our will is not to be forced into cooperation with divine agencies, but it must be voluntarily submitted. Were it possible to force upon you with a hundredfold greater intensity the influence of the Spirit of God, it would not make you a Christian, a fit subject for Heaven. The stronghold of

> *Satan would not be broken. The will must be placed on the side of God's will. You are not able, of yourself, to bring your purposes and desires and inclinations into submission to the will of God; but if you are 'willing to be made willing,' God will accomplish the work for you, even 'casting down imaginations, and every high thing that exalteth itself against the knowledge of God, and bringing into captivity every thought to the obedience of Christ.' 2 Corinthians 10:5. Then you will 'work out your own salvation with fear and trembling. For it is God Which worketh in you both to will and to do of His good pleasure' Philippians 2:12, 13."[26]*

God's nature dwelling in you will keep you from having any desire to tell that lie. Does that mean Satan won't tempt? Absolutely not! He will tempt, and will tempt as much as he can, just as he continually tempted Christ—so much in fact that it could be said that Christ was "in all points tempted like as we are," fortunately, "yet without sin" (Hebrews 4:15).

Perhaps you ask, "When does temptation become sin?" Is it when we succumb to the evil suggestion and act on it? No! Are you shocked by my answer? Well, when do we sin? When we let our minds dwell upon the suggestion. Let me put it another way: Temptation becomes sin when we contemplate it! Proverbs 23:7 says, "As a man thinketh in his heart, so is he." Where, then, is the sin? In the heart! To eradicate the act, sin must first be eradicated from the heart. If my heart is clinging to a sin, but I find a way to resist the temptation, I'm only being hypocritical. Why? I'm doing something that I'm not. Someone said, "Restrained badness is the worst kind of goodness." Did you know that restrained badness is the kind of goodness the world expects? The world says, "Don't do this or that where people can see you." Apparently sin is okay if no one else knows about it. Was restrained badness the kind of goodness Jesus was referring to when He said, "Keep My commandments"? I don't think so. Jesus said, "If ye keep My commandments, ye shall abide in My love; even as I have kept My Father's commandments, and abide in His love" (John 15:10).

"That My Joy Might Remain in You"

"These things have I spoken unto you, that My joy might remain in you, and that your joy might be full" (John 15:11).

We could easily spend another evening on what we've been talking about, because it is so hard for us to grasp the power that comes through the indwelling presence of Christ. Do you realize that Jesus doesn't want you going through life restraining badness, but experiencing the power that comes through His indwelling? Now Jesus adds, "These things have I spoken unto you,"—I've counseled you, I've guided you, I've told you these things—"that My joy might remain in you."

In Jesus' day, they didn't understand His joy, and I don't think we understand His joy any better in our day. In our day joy is often equated with frivolity, and we think of a "slaphappy" person. We admire people who are silly, we like people who create laughter, and in fact sometimes describe these people as the "life of the party." That's what we call joy.

But Christ's joy was different. His joy drew little children to come and sit on His lap, for they were naturally attracted to Him and His authentic love. The adults of His day were also attracted by His love, regardless of their culture, their standing, their gender, or any other cultural dividing line that might have existed. Desiring Him, they went from place to place to find and be with Him. Why? Because they were attracted by His love, because they were attracted by His joy. The joy that attracted them to Jesus was the kind He referred to when He said, "That My joy might remain in you." (John 15:11)

What, then, was Christ's joy? It was seeing people recognize in Him the reflection of His Father—something they weren't seeing in anyone else—and knowing He was accomplishing His Father's will for Him. His joy wasn't ego-centered. No, it was all about reflecting His Father's image. Our joy will come in the same way: reflecting the image of Jesus. So Jesus accordingly asks, "Would you like to experience the joy that comes from reflecting My image?"

The Church and the Image of Jesus

We have a bit of a quandary here: seeking this joy, but seeking it in the wrong way, which is an ongoing challenge. Too often, when hearing Jesus' call, we respond by going out, knocking on doors, asking people if they are Christians, and inviting them to study the Bible with us. That's our usual way of responding, and please understand there is nothing wrong with visiting our neighbors and studying the Bible with them—in fact, everything is right about it. But that's not what reflecting the image of Jesus is all about!

Perhaps I am exaggerating here, but I think we primarily approach reflecting the image of Jesus as an activity. What was the early church up to when they were doing God's work? Their one supreme object was to reflect the image of Jesus—that's all—and do whatever they could to further God's work. It wasn't a matter of members being coerced to do this or that, committees mandating some activity, or the apostles using some spiritually-contrived artificial pressure to get the members out. No, their supreme object was reflecting the image of Jesus and doing whatever they could to further the work of God. God performed a miracle in their hearts that enabled them to do just that, and they did it in a manner and with a sense of urgency that far exceeded anything human coercion or pressure could have effected.

It might help if we pause for a few moments and consider the church—and I want to say at the outset that I do this reverently because Jesus died for the church and loved the church with a supreme love in spite of the church's imperfection. The message to the Laodicean church found in Revelation 3:14-21 includes a less than wonderful description: wretched, miserable, blind, poor, and naked. Unfortunately, the church doesn't even recognize its true condition. The description in Revelation 3 is unflattering, but it is God's pronouncement of us, and we shouldn't get upset or discouraged by reading it; just recognize that we've gotten ourselves into a mess as human beings. Fortunately, the same message that accurately describes our condition also enumerates God's remedy. What is it? Christ's robe of righteousness, which covers our nakedness and which constitutes that perfect provision which has in it "not one thread of human devising"![27]

Enjoying Life to the Full

Now Jesus said He wants us to have His joy. What is that joy? Real joy is living and enjoying life to its maximum potential, something that is only possible in the abiding relationship. However, no one, and I mean this from the bottom of my heart, no one can have the joy Jesus was speaking of while going against any of the principles of God's Word which are known to be right—it can't be done; it's utterly impossible. The person who is going against his conscience is only making himself miserable.

Let me get more specific: The individual who hangs onto even one thought that is not based on the Word of God and His truth is walking down a roadway to misery, heartache, and complete destruction, the final outcome of which will be death. What will it take for us to learn this lesson? How is it that the Devil can come along and subtly—"brazenly" is a better descriptor when you consider the controversy that is going on—allure us down the wrong pathway and suggest it won't matter? How did Jesus respond to Satan's suggestions? Did He risk hanging onto any prop—in His case, perhaps supernatural power or personal desire? No! Did He hang onto anything? No. He didn't hang onto even one thing. What did He do? He completely submitted Himself to carrying out one mission: reflecting the image of His Father's character in a world that didn't know Him. Jesus asks us to do the very same thing.

A Final Thought

In closing, we find a sobering thought in *Christ's Object Lessons* that is suggested by Mark 4:29:

"When the fruit is brought forth, immediately He putteth in the sickle, because the harvest is come" (Mark 4:29).

What is being talked about here? Fruit—fruit that comes as a result of abiding. It says the branch abides in the Vine until it bears fruit, and when the fruit emerges, He immediately puts in the sickle, for the harvest has come.

"Christ is waiting with longing desire for the manifestation of Himself in His church. When the character of Christ shall be perfectly reproduced in His people, then He will come to claim them as His Own."[28]

Notes:

[21] White, E.G., Christ Object Lessons, (Washington, D.C.: Review and Herald Publishing Association, 1941), pp. 120, 121.
[22] Ibid., p.120.
[23] Ibid., p. 271.
[24] Ibid., p. 120.
[25] Ibid.
[26] Ellen G. White, *Thoughts From the Mount of Blessing* (Mountain View, Calif.: Pacific Press Publishing Association, 1928), pp. 141-143.
[27] *Christ's Object Lessons*, p. 311.
[28] *Christ's Object Lessons*, p. 69.

Study Questions:

1. Who have we been called to represent and why? What will result? (66,67)

2. During the early church era, what did the people see in the members that was so alluring? (67)

3. Contrast the world's understanding of love with "benevolent" love? (66)

4. What was the primary objective of the church of Ephesus? (68)

5. How does the world label people who have chosen to follow Jesus and how do you feel about that? (70)

6. If victory does not come through resolve and struggle, how does it come? (73)

7. What kind of joy was Jesus referring to when He spoke of His joy being in us? (75)

8. What kind of life is possible when we experience true joy as a result of abiding in the Vine? (76,77)

9. What is the pathway to misery and destruction? (77)

CHAPTER 6

ABIDING AND UNLIMITED JOY

"As the Father has loved Me, so have I loved you: continue ye in My love. If ye keep My commandments, ye shall abide in My love; even as I have kept My Father's commandments, and abide in His love. These things have I spoken unto you, that My joy might remain in you, and that your joy might be full. This is my commandment, That ye love one another, as I have loved you" (John 15:9-12).

Introductory Thoughts

Last time we concentrated on John 15:9, where the disciples learned that God made Jesus His personal Representative for the purpose of revealing love, and His character of love, to the entire universe. God—we are speaking of the "Triune God" (or what many call the Trinity)—needed such a representation, and was going to succeed or fail on the basis of the manifestation of Himself in the life of Jesus, a responsibility that Jesus carried by Himself.

We also learned that Jesus has placed a similar representational responsibility on us. Just as Jesus represented God to the universe, so we are to represent Jesus to our fellow men. Jesus has commissioned us for this role in spite of our sinfulness, weakness, and frailty. Fortunately, He has assigned our task and told us precisely how to execute it.

Describing His Own role, Jesus told the disciples He had been sent to accomplish the will of the Father. Regarding our role, Jesus said, I'm sending you the same way My Father sent Me. Fundamental to the way the Father sent Jesus, was Jesus' continued dependence on His Father. As a result Jesus could say, "Of Myself I can do nothing." So the Bible says, "God was in Christ, reconciling the world unto Himself" (2 Corinthians 5:19). In the same way, Jesus is presently in this world through His human representatives and is choosing us to be His representatives in the same way the Triune God chose Him to represent them to the universe. That's why Jesus said, "You have not chosen Me, but I have chosen you" (John 15:16)!

Reflect for a moment on what it meant for God to make Jesus His Representative, and what it means for Jesus to make us His representatives. If you were to select a person to represent you such that the authority of your name could be used for any purpose, what level of confidence would you need to place in that person? Complete confidence! Complete confidence is what God placed in Jesus, and complete confidence is what Jesus places in us. As a result, Jesus could say, "If ye shall ask anything in My name, I will do it" (John 14:14). I've thought about that many times, because it is like an ambassador being sent to a foreign country and using the authority vested in his sovereign's name to transact any and all business. When we use the name of the Lord Jesus Christ, we are enjoying the same privileges, and operating under the same mandates, as that ambassador.

The Commandment and Abiding

"As the Father has loved Me, so have I loved you: continue ye in My love. If ye keep My commandments, ye shall abide in My love; even as I have kept My Father's commandments, and abide in His love. These things have I spoken unto you, that My joy might remain in you, and that your joy might be full. This is My commandment, That ye love one another, as I have loved you" (John 15:9-12).

These verses belong together and provide much to ponder.

Jesus first said, "If ye keep My commandments, ye shall abide in My love." Then skipping to verse 12 we read, "This is My commandment, That ye love one another." This is the chain of command—the chain of love—that envisions God revealing Himself through Christ, and Christ revealing Himself through us. It was necessary for God to reveal His character of love because Satan had successfully intimated that, instead of God being love, He was actually a phony, an unloving despot, in spite of assertions otherwise. To meet the challenge, Jesus was sent to reveal God's love, and in the process of revealing that love, gave Himself completely. The greatest manifestation of that love was at Calvary, but Calvary was a long time ago, and God needs representatives that will reflect His love in the same way, and to the same degree, in our day.

Jumping to verse 13, Jesus added the following thought: "Greater love hath no man than this, that a man lay down his life for his friends."

This is an important consideration because more times than not we think giving one's physical life for another person is the epitome of love. I would propose that this verse refers to something more, for it is actually easy for a person to give his or her physical life, and even be proud of doing so; and many men and women have willingly taken the deathblow for the sake of love. Is this what Jesus was talking about? No, He wasn't talking about that kind of thing at all.

Two Kinds of Life

It's helpful to note that the word "life" that Jesus was using here is *psuche* in the Greek, and refers to "animal" or "natural" life. By way of contrast, *zoe* is what I term "active" life. Both have breath connected with them, but they are entirely different. The first is the natural or animal life; the other is the active, physical life.

Turn with me to Matthew 10:38, 39, where the word *psuche* is used, and refers to the animal life.

> *"He that taketh not his cross, and followeth after Me, is not worthy of Me. He that findeth his life shall lose it: and he that loseth his life for My sake shall find it."*

It is interesting that Jesus connects the person dying to self with the cross. We often assume that the cross always refers to an event that happened to Jesus, but it may surprise you to learn that Jesus, when speaking of the cross, always referred to it as our cross and not His. He said,

> *"If any man will come after Me, let him deny himself, take up his cross daily, and follow Me"* (Luke 9:23).

What cross was Jesus referring to? It was the cross of dying to self! What cross did Jesus bear? The same cross: death to self! We read that keeping His glory veiled was the most difficult thing that Jesus undertook. Can you see, then, that it was as difficult for Jesus to live on the level of humanity as it is for us to live on the level of divinity?

Now turn with me to Matthew 16:24, 25, where Jesus repeats:

> *"If any man will come after Me, let him deny himself, and take up his cross, and follow Me. For whosoever will save his life shall lose it: and whosoever will lose his life for My sake shall find it."*

The word "life" in verse 25 is *psuche*, the animal or natural life into which we are born.

Jesus told some Greeks about the necessary outcome of the animal nature when He said,

> *"Except a corn of wheat fall into the ground and die, it abideth alone" (John 12:24).*

He was telling them that the natural self had to die. Paul would later tell the Corinthians that we become new creatures in Christ (2 Corinthians 5:17). What did Paul mean by this? Did he mean a partial change? No. He asserted that when a man or woman is born again—when the death he was referring to actually takes place—we become new creatures, from the soles of our feet to the top of our heads. That doesn't mean the old man won't show up occasionally, or that we will never stumble; but his appearance only proves that Satan understands the old animal nature and knows how to produce circumstances and situations that are calculated to bring about our downfall.

In the context of what we have learned about *psuche*, we can then appropriately translate the verse as follows: "Whoever shall save his animal nature shall lose the natural man, and will be completely lost! But whoever shall lose His *psuche* and is born again for My sake, shall find it—which is what the new birth, and the discovery of the need for it, and the complete surrender to the Lord Jesus Christ, is all about.

Another Kind of Commandment

Returning to John 15:10 and Jesus' words, "If ye keep My commandments," we are immediately reminded of the Old Testament commandments—the "Thou shalt have no other Gods before Me" commandments—and the rest of the imperatives given through Moses. Is this what Jesus was talking about? They are part of it, but there is more, for Jesus clarified Himself in John 15:12 when He said, "This is My commandment, That ye love one another, as I have loved you." Christ was speaking of what happens when we abide in His love, and of His desire that we reflect the love that we have experienced in the abiding relationship to our fellow men. Love is the central theme here, however He places the word love in even more endearing terms in verse 13 and onward, when He associates it with the word "friends."

A New Friendship and Joy

The word "friends" comes from the Greek word *philos* and derives from the same root as love, referring to a love that is authentic and true. For example, when we speak of "loved ones," we are primarily referring to relatives. If we speak of "loved ones at home," we are talking about our own family members, not friends who have dropped by. Keeping in mind the Greek *philos* background, becoming "friends,"—becoming sons and daughters of God's family through the adoption process—takes on new meaning. So Jesus was not only talking about the Vine and the branches, and the abiding relationship and fruit-bearing, but He was also saying that if we do these things and abide in His love, we will actually become His "friends."

In John 15:11 we learn about the outcome of the relationship: "These things have I spoken unto you, that My joy might remain in you, and that your joy might be full." Who would have ever thought that the recipe for joy and happiness could be enumerated in such a simple formula? People seek joy in every way —producing things, pursuing materialism, developing a wide circle of friends, going after self-centered aspirations—but not in following His recipe for complete joy.

Sorrow Makes Way for This Joy

Notice John 16:21, 22:

"A woman when she is in travail hath sorrow, because her hour is come: but as soon as she is delivered of the child, she remembereth no more the anguish, for joy that a man is born into the world."

This is an interesting thought so far as physical life is concerned, for it illustrates the new birth process as regards the death of the old man and the birth of the new man.

Verse 22 continues:

> *"And ye now therefore have sorrow: but I will see you again, and your heart shall rejoice, and your joy no man taketh from you."*

Here we are told of a joy that cannot be taken away. What brings this joy? Abiding in the Vine; abiding is the only thing that maintains this joy. "In the world," Jesus said, "ye shall have tribulation" (John 16:33). This is not surprising, since we immediately find ourselves back in the world if we are cut off from the Vine. This doesn't mean that abiding in the Vine will somehow cause us to escape the physical world, but it does mean that we can be in the world but not of the world, as we maintain the *abiding* relationship. Let me restate that: Though we must live in the world, it doesn't mean that we live the way the world lives. Being born again changes how we live in the world, and modifies the kind of joy we experience; and the joy that brims up in our hearts as a result, can't be taken away under any circumstance.

The question might be asked, "Why do we so often lose our joy?" Is it because someone has taken it away? We like to blame other people when we become unhappy, but is it their fault? Have you ever blamed your spouse for something? Notice what Jesus said in John 16:22-24:

> *"And ye now therefore have sorrow: but I will see you again, and your heart shall rejoice, and your joy no man taketh from you. And in that day ye shall ask Me nothing. Verily, verily, I say unto you, Whatsoever ye shall ask the Father in My name, He will give it you. Hitherto have ye asked nothing in My name: ask, and ye shall receive, that your joy may be full."*

Conditions and Prayer

What was Jesus referring to when He said "hitherto?" He was saying, "Up to this point, up to now, you have 'asked nothing in My name'" (John 16:24). Analyzing this, we find help in John 15:16, where He said,

"Ye have not chosen Me, but I have chosen you, and ordained you, that ye should go and bring forth fruit, and that your fruit should remain: that whatsoever ye shall ask of the Father in My name, He may give it you."

Notice the little word "may" that comes at the end of this verse. Why does Jesus say "may"? He's reminding us that asking and receiving of the Father depends on certain conditions being met. In other words, God can only respond to our request if we prepare the way, and there is only one way. And what is that one way? Meeting His conditions! What are these conditions? Combining John 15:16 and John 16:23, 24, we find a glorious blanket promise that includes anything and everything, without reservations. Notice the following statement:

"But to pray in Christ's name means much. It means that we are to accept His character, manifest His spirit, and work His works. The Saviour's promise is given on condition. 'If ye love Me,' He says, 'keep My commandments.' He saves men, not in sin, but from sin; and those who love Him will show their love by obedience."[29]

Praying in Christ's Name

"To pray in Christ's name means much."[30] Recall that Jesus had said that up to that particular moment they had not asked in His name. I wonder, Have we ever asked, really asked, in Jesus' name? "To pray in Christ's name means much. It means that we are to accept His character." What's that? His character of love. That's what we call sanctification, which is the practical impartation of the character of Christ, and is what God wants to do for us. Sanctification follows justification, includes the crediting of His character to our account, and continues the rest of our lives as God keeps giving, and we keep receiving, the character of Jesus Christ.

Continuing, "To pray in Christ's name means much. It means that we are to accept His character, manifest His Spirit [—it gets harder as we go; I would suggest more beautiful, but also more binding upon us—] "and work His works." What was His work? Reflecting the love of God. What should be our work? Reflecting the love of Jesus. That's why He said, "This is My commandment, That ye love one another" (John 15:12).

It all comes back to this matter of love. If we have this love we will be abiding, because it is impossible to reflect this love and not abide. Jesus said, "Abide in Me, and I in you. As the branch cannot bear fruit of itself, except it abide in the vine; no more can ye, except ye abide in Me" (John 15:4). The branch must receive love from the Vine in order to reflect love. It cannot be manufactured; it cannot come from anything but the genuine stock. So we are told, "To pray in Christ's name means much. It means to accept His character, manifest His Spirit, and work His works." This "anything" promise is genuine, but it is given on condition of the love that we have been studying about.

Perhaps you are asking, "What does this mean on a practical basis?" It means surrendering to the Lord, accepting Him because we recognize our need, and saying "Lord, please enter, I accept You." If we are praying honestly, if we are willing to accept His character, if we are willing to live His life and do His work, then we can pray in the name of Jesus as He encouraged His disciples to do, and have *every* expectation of obtaining the answer.

Now, why did Jesus say that the disciples had not been praying in His name prior to that time? Because they had not felt the need to do so up to then. Though they cherished His physical presence and sought to be close to Him, though they felt uncomfortable away from Him, they were wholly unacquainted with the need of His indwelling presence. They didn't know about the need to be born again any more than Nicodemus knew about it. Though the disciples had been with Jesus a long time, they still didn't understand. I wonder if things have changed very much in our day? Though many of us have been members of the church for a long time, we sadly neither understand the need to be born again nor the need to have the old animal nature die.

Chosen by the Vine

Jesus followed up, saying in John 15:16:

> *"Ye have not chosen Me, but I have chosen you, and ordained you, that ye should go and bring forth fruit, and that your fruit should remain."*

The only way fruit can remain is if the branch abides in the Vine. Why is this? Because the branch is continually growing and producing fruit. And the same kind of fruit will be produced day after day. We won't be looking for cherries one day and peaches the next. No, every time we go to that tree we will find the same kind of fruit, even if the fruit is in a different stage of development. And it is in the context of producing fruit that Jesus says, "Whatsoever ye shall ask of the Father in My name, He may give it you" (John 15:16).

Four Great Incentives

What a wonderful thing it would be if our eyes could be opened to really understand what it means to abide in Christ and to experience the blessings that come through abiding. Meade MacGuire's *Life of Victory* suggests four great incentives—objectives might be another way to put it—for seeking the abiding experience:

1. We will stop sinning.

"Whosoever abideth in Him sinneth not: whosoever sinneth hath not seen Him, neither known Him" (1 John 3:6).

It is only when we abide in Christ that we cease sinning. It's impossible for the abiding Christian to commit sin. This abiding experience results in freedom from sin. It doesn't mean temptation will disappear, nor does it mean there won't be an occasional stumble or fall; but it does mean we are not going to deliberately turn our backs on the Lord Jesus if we are abiding in the Vine. Satan may come along with something very attractive, but if we continue abiding in the Vine, the attraction will pass—God will take responsibility for that. All the while the character of the Lord Jesus will continue to be credited to us so long as we are abiding, even if we make an unintentional mistake. Intentional rebelliousness that proceeds out of an unborn natural heart that hasn't yet died will be past history. Jesus says that being born again and abiding will take care of this.

2. We will bring forth fruit.

> "He that abideth in Me, and I in him, the same bringeth forth much fruit: for without Me ye can do nothing" (John 15:5).

The fruit we have been studying, the fruit of the Spirit, is the fruit of the character of Jesus that God reproduces in us, and keeps coming as the branch continually receives sap from the Vine. If we cease abiding, this sap will stop flowing, and the character will be marred.

3. We will enjoy success in prayer.

> "If ye abide in Me, and My words abide in you, ye shall ask what ye will, and it shall be done unto you" (John 15:7).

If we abide, we can expect to produce the fruit of God's character in our lives. As Jesus bore the fruit of the Father, so we will produce the fruit of Jesus Christ—the branch will bear the same kind of fruit as the Vine! If the vine is a grapevine, there's going to be grapes; you won't find peaches! God has ordained the simple abiding process to bring about the right kind of fruit—the fruit of God's character. This is a truly simple process.

4. We will not be ashamed at His coming.

> "And now, little children, abide in Him; that, when He shall appear, we may have confidence, and not be ashamed before Him at His coming" (1 John 2:28).

What a glorious privilege to know that as we abide in the Lord Jesus we don't need to fear His coming; rather, we can look forward with confidence—with joy and gladness, with great anticipation—to His Second Coming.

Now this does not mean that we will not stumble and fall, but it does mean that we will not deliberately turn our backs on Jesus and sin. There may be mistakes; the devil may come along with some blight-causing attraction, but it will pass away for Jesus will take care of that. Your record will continue to read that the character of God is yours—that character will be credited to you even if you make an unintentional mistake. This speaks to the difference between sin and sins, the difference between intentional rebelliousness that comes out of the natural heart and life that has not been born again and needs to die, and unintentional mistakes that can come as we are seeking to abide in Christ. Abiding in Christ the natural man is taken care of.

A Glorious Conclusion

God wants us to have this kind of confident experience on a daily basis. As Meade MacGuire put it,

> "In this abiding experience lies our daily victory over sin, our ability to bring forth to His glory, our unlimited success in prayer, and our assurance of being ready to meet our King when He returns in glory."[31]

These are God's great incentives for pursuing the abiding experience.

Prayer

Our Heavenly Father, we have been touching some of the most critical and important truths that your Word contains, for truly it speaks the truth when it says that without You, we can do nothing. Lord, we are helpless—totally helpless. As a branch cut off from its source of life simply withers and is only fit for the fire, so we are only fit for the fire unless we abide in You. Lord, may we realize this more and more every day. May we rely upon You, trust You, believe You, and appropriate Your Word in our lives, so that we might bear fruit. May that fruit, dear Lord, be the fruit of the Spirit—love, joy, peace, long-suffering, gentleness, goodness, patience, temperance—these characteristics, Lord, that we need so badly if we are to reflect Your character to a world that needs to see them, especially in God's people, that they might be drawn to Christ through us. Hear our prayer. Thank You, dear Lord, for listening to us; and we ask for all of these blessings in the name of Jesus, Who died, rose again, and is our Saviour at this moment. We pray and ask all these things in His name. Amen.

Notes:

[29] Ellen G. White, *The Desire of Ages* (Boise: Pacific Press Publishing Association, 1898, 1940), p. 668.
[30] Ibid.
[31] Meade MacGuire, *The Life of Victory* (Washington, D.C.: Review and Herald Publishing Association, 1924), p. 154.

Study Questions:

1. What was Jesus referring to when He spoke of the cross? (83)

2. What did Jesus mean when He referred to His disciples as His friends? (85)

3. What is Jesus' complete recipe for joy? (85)

4. What does it mean to pray in Christ's name? (87)

5. What four great incentives will motivate us to seek the abiding experience? (89,90)

HELPFUL LINKS ON THE INTERNET:

Ellen White Estate:
www.ellengwhite.org (download materials)

Path to Prayer - Dan Augsburger:

www.path2prayer.com or email: path2prayer@yahoo.com

Hope Video Ministries:
www.hopevideo.org (audio and video sermons)

David Gates:
www.gospelministry.org (sermons and books)

The Crucified Walk:
www.thecrucifiedwalk.com (bible studies)
thecrucifiedwalk@gmail.com
(907)764-4921

Justified Walk Ministries:
If you would like the complete sermon series on CD
www.justifiedwalk.com (see below)
justifiedwalk@justifiedwalk.com

For our address and phone number (see copywrite page)
All materials are free of charge and download for free from the internet.

Other materials available from Justified Walk Ministries:

His Robe or Mine in other languages and English large print:
Spanish, Portugese, Chinese, Malagasy, French, Korean, Russian and Romanian. German and Dutch are being translated. If you would like to translate this book into your language please call Justifiedwalk Ministries.

Dying to self websites in other languages:

Chinese: www.xinxiangyuan.com
You can find the series listed below on the web at www. justified-walk.com. You can listen to them on-line or download them. You can also find the associated handouts for the Justified Walk series as downloadable pdf files. This book, His Robe Or Mine, is also available as a downloadable pdf file.

The Justified Walk series,
(9 sermons on-line, CD, Cassette, MP3)
The Justified Walk handout materials, (on-line & pdf)

Righteousness By Faith series,
(10 sermons on-line, MP3)

His Robe or Mine
(on-line, pdf and print)

The Branch & The Vine series,
(6 sermons on-line, CD, etc..)

God's Last Effort by Dart (the little red book)
(online and in print)

New Sermon Series available:
The Atonement (Audio 13 part series online, CD)
Child Guidance (Audio CD and soon online!)
The Cross of Christ (3 part series, CD)
Along with other sermons from speakers who expound on the dying to self message.

May God richly bless you as you share this message and these materials with others. To help them gain the saving knowledge and heart experience you have found in this message through God.